Ultimate Travel Guide To

Sayulita,

MEXICO

Sayulita Secrets Revealed:
The Travel Guide You Can't Miss!

Elizabeth Whyte

COPYRIGHT NOTICE

SCAN TO SEE ALL MY BOOKS

DISCLAIMER

Please note that the information contained within this document is for educational purposes only. The information contained herein has been obtained from sources believed to be reliable at the time of publication. The opinions expressed herein are subject to change without notice.

Readers acknowledge that the Author / Publisher is not engaging in rendering legal, financial or professional advice. The Publisher / Author disclaims all warranties as to the accuracy, completeness, or adequacy of such information.

The Publisher assumes no liability for errors, omissions, or inadequacies in the information contained herein or from the interpretations thereof. The publisher / Author specifically disclaims any liability from the use or application of the information contained herein or from the interpretations thereof.

TABLE OF CONTENT

Appendix

Introduction

WELCOME TO SAYULITA, MEXICO!

Sayulita, Mexico's magnificent Pacific coast, emerges as a treasure that beckons guests seeking a genuine blend of surf, sun, and vivid culture. This introduction is your ticket to an adventure that promises not just sandy beaches and turquoise oceans, but also an immersive journey into the heart of a vibrant bohemian town. Welcome to the Ultimate Sayulita Travel Guide, your guide to navigating the beauty and attraction of this seaside paradise.

Welcome to Sayulita

The rhythmic lull of the waves, the warm embrace of tropical breezes, and the brilliant hues of a town that exemplifies the essence of laid-back luxury meet you as you arrive onto the sun-kissed shores of Sayulita.

Welcome to a resort that combines the tranquility of a coastal getaway with the vivacity of a bustling city. Sayulita has an unmistakable magnetic pull that attracts travelers from all over the world, and as you explore its cobblestone alleyways and sandy corners, you'll quickly find the distinct spirit that makes this town an outstanding destination.

Sayulita's inviting ambiance extends beyond its natural beauty; it can be found in the residents' smiles, the unique art that adorns every corner, and the aroma of wonderful street cuisine drifting through the air. Sayulita extends its arms wide to embrace you in an experience that exceeds the ordinary, whether you're an experienced surfer looking for the perfect wave or a culture enthusiast ready to explore the vibrant tapestry of Mexican life.

Why Sayulita?

"Why Sayulita?" is a question with as many answers as there are people in the town. Sayulita is more than a destination; it's a tapestry of experiences woven together by natural, cultural, and adventurous threads. Surfers go to its world-class breaks, families seek refuge in its friendly community, and artists find inspiration in its bohemian appeal.

Sayulita, beyond the charm of its magnificent beaches, provides a look into traditional Mexican life. During local festivals, the town's heart beats to the rhythm of traditional music, and its streets come alive with brilliant colors. Sayulita's allure stems not just from what it has to offer, but also from how it makes you feel—like a visitor discovering a hidden refuge that exceeds the traditional tourist experience.

The answer to the question "Why Sayulita?" is found in its rich cultural legacy, where indigenous traditions coexist with contemporary craftsmanship. The community's warm embrace welcomes guests, asking them to share in the simplicity of life on the Pacific coast.

About This guide

This detailed guide to Sayulita is meant to reveal the town's treasures and make your journey as smooth as the ebb and flow of the Pacific tide. This guide is more than just a collection of data; it is a crafted narrative that captures the heart of Sayulita, providing insights that go beyond ordinary travel brochures.

Inside, you'll find a plethora of information ranging from practical travel and lodging advice to in-depth investigations of local culture, cuisine, and adventure. We made an effort to create a handbook that caters to all types of vacationers, whether you're a thrill-seeker looking for the perfect wave or a leisurely explorer soaking up the rays.

How to Use This Guide

To get the most out of your Sayulita vacation, learn how to use this guide successfully. Here's a road map to help you make the most of the information available to you:

- **Chapter Navigation:** The guide is divided into chapters, each of which is dedicated to a different component of your Sayulita adventure. Use the table of contents to navigate to the parts that interest you, whether they are about planning, activities, dining, or practical information.

- **Subsections & Details:** Subsections go into certain themes inside each chapter. These offer deep insights, ideas, and insider tips to help you better understand and enjoy Sayulita.

- **Practical Advice:** Look for practical advice and ideas strewn throughout the guide. From language suggestions to safety measures, these tidbits of information are intended to make your trip experience more pleasurable and smoother.

- **Maps and Visual Aids:** Visual learners will appreciate the strategically placed maps, photos, and illustrations that supplement the textual content. Use these tools to help you envision locations, comprehend layouts, and plan your trip.

- **Appendix and Index:** Don't forget to look through the appendix for important materials such as useful phrases, packing lists, and supplementary maps. The index at the end of the handbook can be used to quickly locate specific material.

Allow curiosity to be your guide and spontaneity to be your companion as you go through the pages of the Ultimate Guide to Sayulita.

May this book serve as the key to unlocking the plethora of treasures that Sayulita has to offer, guaranteeing that your experience on the Pacific coast is nothing short of remarkable.

Chapter 1

PLANNING YOUR TRIP

A trip to Sayulita necessitates careful planning in order to get the most of this coastal beauty. Chapter 1 is your entry point into smart trip planning, discussing critical factors such as the best time to come and the lively festivals that paint the town with colors and celebrations.

When Is the Best Time to Visit?

Choosing the best time to visit Sayulita is a critical decision that will have a massive impact on your experience. Sayulita, which is bathed in everlasting summer, welcomes visitors all year, with each season bringing a particular flavor of the town's attractiveness.

Seasonal Considerations

- **High Season (November to April):** Also known as the dry season, this time is distinguished by sunny days and warm nights. High season draws surfers looking for the finest wave conditions, families on vacation, and individuals looking for a break from winter in other areas of the world. During this peak tourist season, expect congested streets, active beaches, and a thriving nightlife.

- **Shoulder Seasons (May to June, September to October):** The shoulder months offer a more relaxed atmosphere as they transition between dry and rainy seasons. Crowds thin, making for a more personal encounter. While small rain showers may occur in May and June, they contribute to the lush foliage that surrounds the area. The rainy season lasts from September to October, with intermittent downpours freshening the town and presenting a distinct perspective of Sayulita.

- **Low Season (July to August):** Summer in Sayulita ushers in the low season, attracting surfers looking for large waves as well as those looking for a tranquil vacation. While rain showers are to be expected, the tropical landscape thrives during this time. This time of the year allows budget-conscious visitors to enjoy the splendor of Sayulita with fewer tourists.

Understanding the intricacies of each season enables you to tailor your vacation to your preferences, whether you prefer the energy of high season or the tranquility of shoulder and low seasons.

Festivals and Events

Aside from weather issues, Sayulita's cultural calendar is jam-packed with festivals and events that will liven up your vacation. Immerse yourself in the local celebrations, each of which offers a unique look into Sayulita's heart.

- **Day of the Dead (Dia de los Muertos):** Day of the Dead is a deeply ingrained Mexican tradition that honors deceased loved ones and is celebrated from late October to early November. Sayulita is transformed into a colorful tapestry with ornate altars, parades, and boisterous festivals. It's a moment when the streets come alive with the spirit of memory and joy.

- **Fiesta Sayulita (January):** This annual event celebrates surf, music, and food. Fiesta Sayulita is a week-long celebration that brings together surfers, artists, and foodies. Enjoy surf competitions, great music, and gourmet cuisine set against the gorgeous beaches of Sayulita.

- **Semana Santa (Holy Week):** Semana Santa is a prominent religious event that takes place in late March or early April. Processions, religious rites, and cultural activities are attended by pilgrims, locals, and visitors. While it can be crowded, enjoying the cultural richness of Semana Santa is an unforgettable feature of a Sayulita visit during this time.

- **Mariachi Festival (December):** Sayulita hosts a Mariachi Festival in December, filling the air with the soul-stirring melodies of traditional Mexican music. This event highlights the abilities of local and international mariachi bands, creating a joyous atmosphere ideal for cultural immersion.

By timing your visit to coincide with these festivals, you will not only experience the colorful atmosphere of Sayulita, but you will also engage with the community in a way that goes beyond the normal tourist experience. Planning your trip around these events allows you to engage with the town's cultural fabric more deeply.

The emphasis in this Chapter is on careful planning, ensuring that the time of your visit corresponds to your tastes and expectations. Sayulita welcomes you with open arms, whether you're looking for the energy of peak season or the tranquility of the shoulder and low seasons.

How to Get There

The journey to Sayulita is an important part of the adventure, and understanding the various factors of getting there is essential for a smooth travel experience. This section digs into modes of transportation, providing information on air travel and ground transportation choices to get you from your starting location to the sun-drenched beaches of Sayulita.

Air Travel

Because of its growing popularity, Sayulita is now easily accessible by air, with the Gustavo Daz Ordaz International Airport (PVR) in Puerto Vallarta serving as the principal gateway. Flying to Sayulita requires a combination of flights and ground transportation to provide a seamless transfer from the airport to the town.

- **Choosing the Right Airport:** When planning your trip, keep Gustavo Daz Ordaz International Airport's convenience and travel alternatives in mind. This airport, about 25 miles south of Sayulita, is well-connected to major cities in the United States, Canada, and other regions of Mexico. American Airlines, Delta, United, and

WestJet all have regular flights to Puerto Vallarta.

- **Ground Transportation from Puerto Vallarta Airport:** Once you arrive in Puerto Vallarta, you have several options for getting to Sayulita. At the airport, taxis, shuttle services, and rental automobiles are readily available. Taxis are a convenient but somewhat more expensive option, but shuttle services offer shared trips, making them a more cost-effective option for solitary travelers or groups. Those seeking to explore the region at their own leisure can benefit from renting a car.

- **Private Transportation Services:** Consider scheduling private transportation services in advance for a more personalized and pleasant experience. Several firms provide dependable and fast private shuttles from the airport to Sayulita, allowing you to relax and enjoy the gorgeous route without having to deal with the hassles of public transit.

- **Local Airlines and Small Airports:** Consider regional airlines and smaller airports if you're flying within Mexico. Tepic International Airport (TPQ) and Licenciado Miguel de la Madrid Airport (CLQ) are both within a comfortable driving distance to Sayulita and offer domestic flights.

Understanding air travel logistics provides a stress-free arrival in Sayulita, laying the groundwork for a pleasant and pleasurable stay.

Ground Transportation

Once you've arrived in Puerto Vallarta or a neighboring airport, you'll need to take ground transportation to Sayulita. This section looks at the numerous options available, each of which provides a unique perspective on the region's beauty and culture.

- **Taxis**: Taxis are easily accessible at the airport and offer a convenient but somewhat more expensive means of transportation. Taxis, which provide door-to-door service, can take you directly to Sayulita. Before you begin your journey, be sure you and the driver have agreed on a fare.

- **Shuttle Services**: Shared shuttle services are a popular and inexpensive way to go from the airport to Sayulita. These services run on a schedule and can accommodate numerous people, making them ideal for lone travelers or small groups. It's best to book these services ahead of time to ensure your spot and avoid any needless delays.

- **Rental cars**: Rental cars are available at the airport for individuals who want flexibility and autonomy. This is the best option for travelers who want to explore the nearby places or have certain plans in mind. Before starting on a self-driving excursion, familiarize yourself with local traffic regulations and road conditions.

- **Private Transportation Services:** Consider scheduling private transportation services for a stress-free journey. Several reliable organizations provide air-conditioned automobiles driven by competent drivers in comfortable vehicles. This option provides a more personalized experience, allowing you to relax and enjoy the gorgeous trip while someone else handles the practicalities.

- **Local Buses:** For those on a tight budget, local busses are an inexpensive way to get from Puerto Vallarta to Sayulita. Buses are available at Puerto Vallarta's major bus terminal and provide a look into local life along the journey.

Navigating ground transportation is an important element of any Sayulita vacation, and your choice can impact the overall tone of your trip. Whether you choose a cab for its convenience, a shared shuttle for its companionship, a rental car for its flexibility, or private transportation for its comfort, each option allows you to immerse yourself in the sights and sounds of the journey.

Consider all the different factors that fit with your tastes as you plan your trip to Sayulita, from the convenience of air travel to the mode of ground transportation that complements your travel style. This careful planning guarantees that your arrival in Sayulita is not only a transition but the start of an amazing vacation on Mexico's Pacific coast.

Entry and Visa Requirements

Navigating visa and entry formalities is an important part of organizing your vacation to Sayulita, Mexico. Understanding the appropriate papers, visa requirements, and entrance processes enables a seamless and trouble-free entry into the nation, enabling you to focus on the exciting pleasures that await you in this seaside paradise.

Mexico Visa Requirements:

Mexico has a comparatively lax visa requirement for many nationalities, making it an accessible destination for visitors from all over the world. The particular requirements, however, may differ based on your country, as well as the purpose and duration of your travel. Here's a high-level overview:

- **Tourist Visa (FMM - Forma Migratoria Múltiple**): Most travelers can enter Mexico using a Tourist Visa for short visits (up to 180 days). This visa, known as the FMM, is available upon arrival by air or land. Airlines generally give it during flights or during border crossings. Fill out the FMM form completely and keep the detachable piece as it will be required upon leaving.

- **Visitor Visa:** If you intend to stay for more than 180 days or engage in particular activities such as business or study, you may need to apply in advance at a Mexican consulate or embassy. This visa will have certain conditions, such as proof of your visit's purpose and financial means to maintain yourself during your stay.

- **Other Visa Categories:** For individuals wishing to stay for an extended amount of time or migrate, Mexico offers a variety of visa categories, including work visas, student visas, and permanent residency opportunities. Each category has its own set of requirements, and applicants should consult with the local Mexican consulate for further details.

Entry Protocols and Documentation:

Aside from visa requirements, it is critical to understand entry protocols and the papers required for a smooth entry into Mexico. Attending to these details helps to minimize unnecessary delays and assures a stress-free arrival.

- **Passport Validity:** Make sure your passport is valid for at least six months beyond your scheduled departure date. Many countries, like Mexico, have this as a standard requirement.

- **Return or Onward Ticket:** Immigration officials may request documentation of a return or onward ticket, confirming that you intend to depart the country within the time frame specified. Typically, having a confirmed flight reservation or itinerary is sufficient.

- **Lodging Confirmation:** While not usually essential, having confirmation of your lodging for at least the first half of your visit might be advantageous. This could be a hotel reservation or an invitation letter from a host.

- **Financial Means:** While it is not usually required, it is prudent to have proof of sufficient finances to cover your stay in Mexico. This might be bank statements, credit cards, or cash.

- **Health Declaration Form**: Due to global health concerns, particularly the continuing COVID-19 pandemic, Mexico may require visitors to complete a health declaration form. Check the most recent Mexican government rules and recommendations, and be prepared to comply with any health and safety restrictions in place.

Understanding the Tourist Card (FMM):

The Tourist Card (FMM) is a necessary document for tourists entering Mexico, and it is usually distributed by airlines during the journey or available at border crossings. It demonstrates that you are legally present in the country for tourism purposes. Here are some key facts concerning the FMM:

- **Stay Duration:** The FMM permits for a stay of up to 180 days. Make sure you understand the actual time limit assigned to you upon arrival, as exceeding it can result in fines or other penalties.

- **Detachable Portion:** The FMM is divided into two sections, one of which can be detached and carried with you. This removable element will be required while exiting the nation, so make sure you don't lose it while you're here.

- **Renewal or Extension:** If you want to stay longer than the initial period, you can look at choices for renewal or extension. It is best to seek advice from the local immigration office or embassy on the process.

Updates and Special Considerations:

Given the ever-changing nature of travel restrictions and global events, it's critical to stay up to date on any modifications or particular concerns regarding Mexico's visa and entry procedures. Before departing on your journey, check for updates from official government sources or consult with the Mexican consulate or embassy in your home country.

Accommodation Options

Choosing the correct place to stay is an important part of arranging your vacation to Sayulita. The town has a wide choice of hotel alternatives to suit a variety of tastes and budgets. Sayulita has it all, whether you like the opulence of a beachside resort, the intimacy of a holiday rental, or the simplicity of camping beneath the stars.

Resorts and Hotels

- **Sayulita Beach House Hotel**

The Sayulita Beach House Hotel, located in the heart of Sayulita, offers a perfect blend of modern comfort and coastal charm. This boutique hotel, located only steps away from the pristine Playa Sayulita, provides convenient access to the town's bustling energy while yet offering a tranquil respite. The hotel has spacious rooms with private balconies, a rooftop patio with spectacular ocean views, and a peaceful pool area.

Location: Delfines 12, Sayulita, Nayarit, Mexico.

- **Hotel Kupuri**

Hotel Kupuri is a refuge of elegance and tranquillity for visitors seeking a sumptuous escape. This boutique hotel is nestled among lush tropical gardens and features spacious suites with contemporary Mexican decor, private terraces, and views of the surrounding hills. Guests can have a spa treatment, relax by the pool, or dine on gourmet food at the on-site restaurant.

Location: Calle Gaviotas 1, Sayulita, Nayarit, Mexico.

- **Villa Amor**

Villa Amor, perched on the cliffs overlooking the Pacific, provides an unforgettable setting for a romantic break or a family retreat. This resort-style hotel offers villas and casitas with traditional Mexican architecture and modern conveniences. Guests can take in breathtaking ocean views while relaxing in infinity pools or dining at the cliffside restaurant.

Location: Camino a Playa Los Muertos S/N, Sayulita, Nayarit, Mexico.

Vacation Rentals

- **Casa Buena Onda**

Vacation rentals like Casa Buena Onda give a home away from home for people looking for a more immersive and personalized experience. With its beautiful garden, outdoor terrace, and private pool, this delightful property in the center of Sayulita offers a calm respite. Families and groups searching for a self-catering option will appreciate the big rooms and fully equipped kitchen.

Location: Calle Miramar 13, Sayulita, Nayarit, Mexico.

- **Sayulita Casitas**

Sayulita Casitas has a variety of vacation rentals, ranging from modest studios to expansive villas, to accommodate varied party sizes and interests. Located within walking distance to the town center and beaches, these casitas have colorful design, well-equipped kitchens, and outdoor spaces, allowing guests to enjoy Sayulita like a native.

Location: Av Revolución 60, Sayulita, Nayarit, Mexico.

- **Casa Dos Chicos**

Casa Dos Chicos is an exceptional vacation home located in the beautiful hills of Sayulita that offers a unique blend of luxury and authenticity. This sprawling home features various cottages, a private pool, and breathtaking ocean views. Casa Dos Chicos offers a quiet refuge without losing convenience, thanks to its modern architecture and accessibility to both the beach and town.

Location: Camino a la Playa Los Muertos, Sayulita, Nayarit, Mexico.

Camping Options

- ## Sayulita Trailer Park & Bungalows

Sayulita Trailer Park & Bungalows is an ideal choice for those looking for a camping experience with enhanced conveniences. This campground, just a short walk from the beach, has RV and tent spaces as well as lovely bungalows with modest facilities. The community kitchen, outdoor seating areas, and proximity to Sayulita's attractions make it an excellent choice for those on a tight budget.

Location: Manuel Navarrete 3, Sayulita, Nayarit, Mexico.

- ## Teitiare Estates

Teitiare Estates provides a one-of-a-kind camping experience set within a private natural reserve. This eco-friendly camping site, nestled in the hills above Sayulita, offers visitors to interact with nature while yet enjoying vital facilities. For a comfortable outdoor stay, guests can camp in personal tents or hire fully-equipped glamping tents. There are additional social areas, a swimming pool, and panoramic views of the surrounding jungle on the property.

Location: Camino a la Playa Los Muertos, Sayulita, Nayarit, Mexico.

- **Camping Sayulita**

Camping Sayulita offers a more rustic camping experience closer to the beach at a lower cost. This campsite is a short walk from Playa Sayulita and offers covered tent spaces, modest toilets, and a shared kitchen. The relaxed environment and proximity to the coast make it popular with backpackers and adventure seekers.

Location: Calle Jose Mariscal, Sayulita, Nayarit, Mexico.

Choosing the Right Accommodation for You:

The best place to stay in Sayulita depends on your interests, budget, and the type of experience you want. Hotels and resorts give convenience and luxury, while vacation rentals offer a more personalized and flexible stay, and camping choices cater to those who wish to get back to nature.

To ensure a wonderful stay in this coastal sanctuary, consider the location, amenities, and environment that correspond to your travel style.

Chapter 2

GETTING TO KNOW SAYULITA

Sayulita, a bustling seaside town on Mexico's Pacific coast, entices visitors with its own blend of surf culture, bohemian appeal, and natural beauty.

Chapter 2 encourages you to explore Sayulita's heart, presenting an overview that includes its rich history, cultural tapestry, and the physical and climatic aspects that define this magnificent destination.

Sayulita Overview

Sayulita, located on the Riviera Nayarit in the state of Nayarit, is a compelling blend of heritage and modernity. Sayulita, formerly a peaceful fishing village, has transformed into a hub that flawlessly blends the laid-back vibes of a beach town with a booming arts scene and a feeling of community that appeals with both locals and visitors.

Cobblestone Streets & colorful Facades: As you walk through Sayulita's streets, the charm of its cobblestone streets and bright facades becomes immediately apparent. The tiny streets are lined with artisan stores, surf boutiques, and open-air cafes, creating a quirky environment that reflects the soul of this seaside town.

Surf Culture and Bohemian Spirit: Sayulita's reputation as a surfing hotspot is deeply embedded in its culture. Surfers from all over the world come to enjoy its steady waves and friendly surf community. The bohemian attitude pervades the air, as evidenced by the bustling art scene, lively festivals, and the unique mix of people that call Sayulita home, even if only for a short time.

Sayulita has managed to maintain a close-knit community atmosphere despite its growing popularity. The locals are friendly, and the small nature of the town encourages contact between inhabitants and visitors. The social vibe is obvious whether you're wandering around the central plaza, attending a local event, or enjoying coffee at a seashore cafe.

Culture and History

Sayulita's Indigenous roots:

Sayulita's history extends back to the pre-Hispanic era, when indigenous groups lived in the area. The early residents included the Cora and Huichol peoples, who had extensive cultural traditions. Evidence of their existence may still be seen in the surrounding hills, where sacred places and ceremonial regions provide insight into the region's original history.

Spanish Influence and Fishing Village Origins:

With the entrance of Spanish explorers in the 16th century, a period of colonization and cultural interaction began. However, it wasn't until the mid-twentieth century that Sayulita began to evolve from a traditional fishing community to a resort famed for its surf breaks and bohemian atmosphere. The inflow of surfers in the 1960s and 1970s was critical in molding Sayulita's identity, launching it into the global spotlight.

Artistic Expression and Cultural Fusion:

Sayulita's cultural landscape exemplifies the blending of indigenous traditions, Spanish influence, and worldwide community manifestations. Murals cover the town's streets, while art galleries display the work of local and international artists. Sayulita's diversified appeal reflects the many influences that have influenced its cultural narrative.

Climate and Geography

The Pacific Playground:

Sayulita is situated along the Pacific coast, roughly 25 miles north of Puerto Vallarta. The hamlet is located along the Riviera Nayarit, which is known for its clean beaches, thick jungles, and various ecosystems. Sayulita is set between the Sierra Madre Occidental mountains and the Pacific Ocean, producing a panorama that combines tropical attractiveness with rough mountain splendor.

Bays and Beaches:

Sayulita's beaches are a major draw, each with its own distinct personality. The main beach, Playa Sayulita, is a hive of activity, with surfers catching waves, beachgoers soaking in the rays, and vendors selling local foods. Playa Los Muertos, to the south, offers a more tranquil retreat with its rocky coves and lovely waves. These beaches, along with others such as Playa Carricitos and Playa Patzcuaro, contribute to Sayulita's unique coastal tapestry.

Climate:

Sayulita has a tropical environment that is distinguished by warm temperatures all year. From November to April, the dry season delivers sunny days and warm evenings, making it the busiest tourist season. From May to October, the town's lush foliage is nourished by rain showers, which contribute to the town's colorful flora. While the wet season is considered the low season for tourists, it provides a distinct perspective of Sayulita, with less visitors and a lush, revitalized landscape.

Nature Trails and Ecological Reserves:

Sayulita is surrounded by ecological reserves and nature paths that highlight the region's biodiversity. A short stroll from town, the Sayulita Ecological Reserve provides an introduction to the region's rich flora and fauna. The Monkey Mountain Trail offers panoramic views of the Pacific and is popular among hikers seeking adventure as well as nature immersion.

Understanding Sayulita's geology and climate allows visitors to tailor their vacation to their preferences, whether they prefer the lively energy of the dry season or the peacefulness of the wet season. Sayulita's allure is enhanced by its beautiful landscapes and various ecosystems, which provide as a backdrop for the diverse adventures that await in this Pacific paradise.

The overview of Sayulita, its history, culture, geography, and climate come together to offer a comprehensive picture of this coastal gem. As you travel to Sayulita, this understanding will serve as a basis for enjoying the town's lively character, rich tradition, and natural beauty, which will set the stage for an outstanding experience on Mexico's Pacific coast.

Districts and Neighborhoods

Sayulita's vibrant and diverse personality is made up of numerous neighborhoods and districts that contribute to the town's special charm. From the bustling town center to the calm beaches and mountains, each area has a distinct feel. This chapter delves into the numerous communities and districts that make up Sayulita's tapestry.

Sayulita Pueblo

Sayulita Pueblo is the town's pulsing center, where the community's vitality converges in a beautiful combination of colors, sounds, and fragrances. The pueblo, or town center, is an enthralling blend of cobblestone walkways, bustling markets, and a central plaza where locals and visitors alike congregate to interact.

Key Features:

- **Central Plaza:** The Plaza Sayulita serves as the town's center point. The plaza, which is lined with stores, restaurants, and bright murals, is a hive of activity. It's a popular venue for gatherings, live music, and festivities.

- **Local Markets:** Sayulita's markets are a sensory feast, with vendors selling fresh vegetables, homemade crafts, and traditional Mexican foods.

On Fridays, the Mercado del Pueblo features local artists and farmers.

- **Art Galleries:** Sayulita Pueblo is covered with vibrant paintings and art installations. Galeria Tanana, for example, exhibits the work of local and international artists, adding to the town's bohemian vibe.

Accommodation:

Sayulita Pueblo is densely packed with boutique hotels and guesthouses that provide easy access to the town's amenities.

Vacation homes in the middle of the city offer an immersive experience, allowing tourists to step out into the bustling atmosphere.

Activities:

- Investigate the central square and its environs.
- Try the local cuisine at a variety of eateries.

- Attend cultural events and festivals in the town center.

Recommended Places to Stay:

Casa Nawalli: A delightful holiday property near the center plaza that combines comfort with proximity to Sayulita's active activity.

Playa Los Muertos

Playa Los Muertos, named after a neighboring cemetery, is a peaceful beach paradise south of Sayulita Pueblo. This location has a calmer vibe, with the sound of crashing waves accompanying guests looking for a peaceful vacation.

Key Features:

- **Scenic beauty:** Playa Los Muertos is famous for its picturesque beauty, which includes golden sands, crystal-clear waters, and rocky outcrops. The beach is surrounded by green hills, making for a gorgeous environment.

- **Iconic Cemetery:** The cemetery near to the beach provides a distinct character to the region. It's a calm and reflective space that adds to the coastal vibe.

Accommodation:

- Beachfront or hillside views are available from boutique hotels and vacation rentals along or near Playa Los Muertos.
- The location caters to people looking for a more isolated and intimate stay away from the bustle of town.

Activities:

- Sunbathing and swimming on the tranquil Playa Los Muertos.
- Explore coastal pathways and vistas with views of the shore.
- Take a contemplative walk-in a nearby cemetery.

Recommended Places to Stay:

Villa Playa Los Muertos: A beachfront property with beautiful views and easy access to the calm Playa Los Muertos.

Gringo Hill

Gringo Hill, which overlooks Sayulita Pueblo, is a residential neighborhood that offers a panoramic view of the town and the Pacific Ocean. The neighborhood is well-known for its elevated houses, beautiful surroundings, and a mix of modern and classic architectural styles.

Key Features:

- **Panoramic Views:** Gringo Hill, with its elevated position, provides some of the most stunning views of Sayulita, with vistas of the town, beaches, and surrounding jungle.

- Gringo Hill, albeit adjacent to the town center, offers a more serene respite away from the pueblo's vibrant environment.

Accommodation:

- Gringo Hill vacation rentals and boutique hotels frequently have infinity pools, terraces, and balconies that take advantage of the breathtaking views.
- This neighborhood caters to individuals looking for a blend of convenience to the town center and a serene hillside environment.

Activities:

- Take leisurely strolls around residential areas and taking in the scenery.
- Take photos of the panoramic vistas of Sayulita and the shoreline.
- Select accommodations with outdoor spaces to enjoy the peace and quiet of the hillside.

Recommended Places to Stay:

Casa Cielo: A hillside vacation rental with panoramic views and a serene hideaway near Sayulita Pueblo and the beaches.

North Sayulita

North Sayulita, which stretches beyond the town center, is distinguished by a mix of residential areas, natural scenery, and access to more quiet beaches. This area in Sayulita has a more tranquil atmosphere while still being close to the town.

Key Features:

- **Secluded beaches:** North Sayulita has less populated beaches, such as Playa Carricitos and Playa Patzcuaro. These beaches provide a more private and tranquil retreat.

- **Nature paths:** Nature paths lead through rainforest environments in the northern borders, providing chances for trekking and wildlife observation.

Accommodation:

North Sayulita vacation rentals and boutique hotels appeal to people wanting a more tranquil setting. Many villas are tucked within the natural surroundings, offering a tropical escape.

Activities:

- Explore isolated beaches for a peaceful day by the sea.
- Hiking or riding through the jungle on natural routes.
- Take part in outdoor activities away from the busy town core.

Recommended Places to Stay:

Villa Sol Blau: A peaceful vacation property surrounded by tropical nature, offering a peaceful stay in North Sayulita.

South Sayulita

South Sayulita combines natural beauty, surfing destinations, and a more easygoing environment. This location is home to some of Sayulita's most famous surf breaks and offers a unique seaside escape.

Key Features:

- **Surfing Spots:** South Sayulita is well-known for its surf-friendly beaches, such as Sayulita Point and Punta Sayulita. Surfers of all levels, from beginners to experts, frequent these spots.

- **Coastal Vistas:** The coastline of South Sayulita is characterized by rocky formations that provide breathtaking views of the Pacific Ocean.

Accommodation:

South Sayulita's boutique hotels and vacation rentals cater to surfers and others looking for a beach escape. Beach access or coastal settings are common features of properties.

Activities:

- Ride the waves at South Sayulita's world-famous surf spots.
- Explore coastal pathways and ocean-viewing vantage points.
- Embrace the relaxed atmosphere at beachfront cafes and pubs.

Recommended Places to Stay:

Casa Olas: A beachfront vacation house with direct access to South Sayulita's surf breakers, providing a great sanctuary for surf fans.

Choosing Your Sayulita Adventure:

Sayulita's neighborhoods and districts provide a variety of experiences, ranging from the busy town center to the peaceful beaches and slopes. Whether you're looking for the bustling energy of Sayulita Pueblo, the serene retreat of Gringo Hill, the hidden charm of North Sayulita, or the surfing paradise of South Sayulita, each location adds to the attractiveness of this coastal hideaway. To choose the best neighborhood for your Sayulita journey, consider your interests, desired activities, and the ambiance that fits your travel style.

Communication and Language

A trip to Sayulita, Mexico, is more than just a physical adventure; it is also a cultural immersion. Understanding the local language and communication nuances enhances your vacation experience by creating connections with the friendly and inviting locals. This chapter explores Sayulita's language environment, including fundamental Spanish phrases and language advice to help you connect with locals.

Basic Spanish Phrases

While English is frequently understood in tourist destinations, making an attempt to communicate in Spanish shows respect for the local culture and can lead to more meaningful relationships. Here are some simple Spanish phrases that will come in handy during your visit to Sayulita:

Greetings and Pleasantries:

- Hello: ¡Hola! (OH-lah)
- Good morning: Buenos días (BWAY-nos DEE-as)
- Good afternoon: Buenas tardes (BWAY-nas TAR-des)
- Good night: Buenas noches (BWAY-nas NOH-chays)
- How are you?: ¿Cómo estás? (KOH-mo es-TAHS)

Common Courtesies:

- Please: Por favor (por fa-VOR)
- Thank you: Gracias (GRAH-syas)
- You're welcome: De nada (day NAH-dah)
- Excuse me: Perdón (PAIR-don)
- I'm sorry: Lo siento (lo SYEN-to)

Navigating Conversations:

- Yes: Sí (see)
- No: No (no)
- Maybe: Tal vez (tall BESS)
- I don't understand: No entiendo (no en-tee-EN-doh)
- Can you help me?: ¿Puedes ayudarme? (PWEH-des a-yoo-DAR-may)

Getting Around:

- Where is...?: ¿Dónde está...? (DOHN-de es-TA)
- Bathroom: Baño (BAH-nyo)
- Beach: Playa (PLAH-ya)
- Town center: Centro del pueblo (SEN-tro del PWEH-blo)

Dining and Food:

- Menu: Menú (meh-NOO)
- Water: Agua (AH-gwa)
- Food: Comida (co-MEE-da)
- Delicious: Delicioso (day-lee-SSOH-so)

- Bill, please: La cuenta, por favor (la KWEHN-ta, por fa-VOR)

Emergency Phrases:

- Help: Ayuda (ah-YOO-dah)
- Doctor: Médico (MAY-dee-co)
- Police: Policía (po-lee-SEE-ah)
- I need assistance: Necesito ayuda (neh-se-SEE-to ah-YOO-dah)

Language Tips for Travelers

Learn Key Phrases Before Your Trip:

Take the opportunity before you arrive in Sayulita to learn some basic Spanish phrases. This not only improves communication but also demonstrates to locals that you value their language and culture.

- **Practice Pronunciation**: Because Spanish pronunciation differs from English pronunciation, speaking essential words aloud helps increase your confidence. Pay attention to accents and syllable emphasis, as these might affect the meaning of words.

- **Embrace Gestures and Body Language:** When language is a barrier, gestures and body language can help to bridge the gap. A nice grin, nod, or simple hand movements can say a lot and aid in the transmission of your message.

- **Use Translation Apps:** Smartphone apps such as Google Translate can be useful for on-the-go translation. While they are not flawless, they can help with understanding and expressing more complex ideas.

- **Consider Basic Spanish Language Classes:** Before your vacation, consider taking basic Spanish language classes. Structured classes can be provided by local community colleges, language learning applications, or online platforms to help you improve your language skills.

- **Communicate in Conversations:** Even if it's only a hello or a simple question, don't be scared to communicate with people in Spanish. Most individuals will appreciate the effort and respond positively.

- **Respect the Local Dialect:** Regional variances in Mexican Spanish exist, and Sayulita is no exception. Accept the local language and any special terms you may encounter during your stay.

- **Ask for Help When Needed:** If you're having trouble communicating, don't be afraid to seek assistance. Locals are generally polite and willing to help, and your efforts to communicate in Spanish will most certainly be rewarded.

- **Be Patient and Open-Minded:** Language obstacles might be difficult to overcome, but patience and an open mind are essential. Enjoy the learning process and the cultural exchange that comes with navigating linguistic differences.

- **Participate in Local Activities:** Take part in local activities, events, or workshops where you can interact with locals. Conversations provided a calm setting for practicing Spanish during these encounters.

Conclusion

Language becomes a bridge in Sayulita, connecting you to the colorful culture and welcoming community. Using simple Spanish phrases and language suggestions improves your trip experience by building genuine connections and a deeper understanding of the rich fabric that distinguishes Sayulita. As you visit the town, take the time to interact with the residents, share tales, and immerse yourself in the language, which will give an added dimension of authenticity to your Sayulita journey.

Chapter 3

ESSENTIAL TRAVEL TIPS

A trip to Sayulita, Mexico, delivers a tapestry of experiences, from sun-drenched beaches to bustling streets brimming with culture and color. To ensure a smooth and rewarding experience, be prepared with vital travel information such as currency and money matters, health and safety precautions, understanding local traditions, and managing Sayulita transit.

Currency and Money matters

Understanding the currency and money situation is essential for a stress-free stay in Sayulita. Understanding the local currency, banking facilities, and ATM availability ensures that you can efficiently manage your finances during your vacation.

Local Currency

The Mexican Peso (MXN) is the country's official currency. There are numerous denominations of peso notes in circulation, as well as centavo coins. While some tourist facilities take major foreign currencies or credit cards, it is best to have Mexican Pesos on hand for transactions, especially at local markets, smaller shops, and cafes.

Currency Exchange Suggestions:

- **Exchange at banks:** Banks provide dependable currency exchange services, and their rates are generally competitive. Before exchanging money, check the current exchange rate and inquire about any costs.

- **Withdrawals from ATMs:** ATMs are widely distributed in Sayulita, making it easy to withdraw Pesos. Keep in mind that ATM withdrawal costs may apply, and currency rates might fluctuate, so check with your bank for overseas transaction fees.

Banking and ATMs

Understanding the financial infrastructure and ATM availability is essential for managing your funds in Sayulita.

Banking Advice:

- **Banking Hours:** Banking hours in Mexico are largely the same as those in the United States, with some banks closing early on Fridays. Plan your visits carefully, particularly if you need to perform banking transactions.

- **Banking:** Major banks, like as Banco Azteca, Bancomer, and Banamex, have local branches in Sayulita. These financial institutions provide a variety of services, such as currency exchange, ATM access, and aid with foreign transactions.

ATM Tips:

- **ATM Locations:** ATMs can be found throughout Sayulita, including numerous in the town center. For a greater choice of services, look for ATMs connected to big worldwide networks.

- **Withdrawal Limits and fees:** ATM withdrawal limits vary, and some machines may impose additional costs. Check with your bank to determine daily withdrawal limits and any fees related with foreign transactions.

Health and Safety

When traveling, it is critical to prioritize your health and safety. Knowing about health precautions, immunizations, and emergency services will help you have a safe and worry-free vacation in Sayulita.

Health Precautions and Vaccinations

It is recommended that you verify and refresh your usual vaccinations before visiting to Sayulita. Vaccinations and health measures particular to the location may also be advised.

Precautions for Health:

- **Water Safety:** While Sayulita's water supply is typically healthy, it's best to consume bottled or purified water to avoid stomach upset.

- **Food Safety:** Enjoy Sayulita's numerous gastronomic options, but be cautious with street food. Choose well-cooked, hot meals and avoid raw or undercooked fish.

- **Sun Protection:** Sayulita's tropical climate brings plenty of sunshine. Pack and use sunscreen on a frequent basis, stay hydrated, and seek shade during high solar hours to avoid sunburn and dehydration.

Vaccinations:

- Ensure that standard immunizations such as measles, mumps, rubella (MMR), diphtheria, pertussis, and tetanus (DPT) are current.

- **Hepatitis A and B:** Get vaccinated against hepatitis A and B, especially if you plan to try local cuisine or participate in outdoor sports.

Emergency Services

Knowing where to find emergency services and healthcare facilities is critical for your safety and peace of mind when visiting Sayulita.

Emergency Services:

- **Medical Emergencies:** The Hospital San Pancho in adjacent San Francisco (San Pancho) provides medical assistance in the event of a medical emergency. In addition, Sayulita's Centro de Salud provides basic healthcare.

- **Emergency Numbers:** In Mexico, dial 911 in an emergency. Put this number on your phone for quick access to police, medical, and fire services.

Travel Insurance:

Comprehensive Coverage: Consider purchasing travel insurance that covers medical emergencies, trip cancellations, and lost or stolen possessions.

Etiquette and Local Customs

Understanding and honoring local customs and etiquette increases your Sayulita cultural experience. Accepting cultural norms and being aware of dos and don'ts help to foster beneficial connections with the community.

Cultural Norms

Like many Mexican municipalities, Sayulita has its own set of cultural conventions that influence daily life and relationships. Understanding these conventions encourages cultural appreciation and mutual respect.

Cultural Tips:

- **Greeting Customs:** A pleasant hug or a warm handshake are traditional ways to greet friends or acquaintances. Use courteous greetings such as "buenas tardes" (good afternoon/evening) and "buenos días" (good morning).

- **Respect for the elderly:** Use formal titles such as "señor" or "señora" to show respect for seniors. As a courtesy, these titles are commonly used to address persons.

- **Religious Customs:** Because Mexico is largely Catholic, religious customs are highly ingrained. Keep local religious practices and customs in consideration, especially during festivals and festivities.

Dos and Don'ts

Understanding cultural dos and don'ts is essential for navigating local norms. Following these rules promotes positive interactions with the community.

Dos:

- **Do Try Local Cuisine:** Experience Sayulita's culinary diversity by sampling local specialties and street food. This not only benefits local businesses but also delivers a taste of authentic Mexican cuisine.

- **Bargain at Markets:** Bargaining is prevalent at local markets. Take pleasure in the process of negotiating pricing while remaining courteous and respectful.

Don'ts:

- **Avoid Offensive Gestures:** Avoid using offensive gestures or expressions. What is accepted in one culture may be insulting in another. Be aware of cultural sensitivities.

- **Don't Litter:** Help preserve Sayulita's natural beauty by disposing of rubbish correctly. Littering is discouraged, and efforts are made to keep the town clean.

Transportation within Sayulita

Navigating Sayulita's transportation choices is vital for touring the town and its surrounds. Understanding your alternatives, from walking the quaint streets to taking public transportation, improves your mobility and overall pleasure.

Getting Around on Foot

Because of Sayulita's small size and pedestrian-friendly streets, strolling is a good method to see the town. Many attractions, restaurants, and beaches are within walking distance, allowing you to take up the bustling environment while also discovering hidden gems.

Walking Tips:

- **Comfortable footwear:** Wear shoes that are comfortable for walking on uneven surfaces, as certain streets in Sayulita are cobblestone.

- **Exploring Neighborhoods:** Walking allows you to immerse yourself in Sayulita's various neighborhoods, from the bustling town center to the quiet beaches and slopes.

Public Transportation

For anyone seeking to venture outside the town limits, Sayulita provides public transportation. Public buses and taxis offer a quick and cost-effective way to travel to local locations.

Tips for Using Public Transportation:

- **Local buses:** Local buses connect Sayulita to adjacent towns and cities. Bus stops are usually in town, and routes can take you to areas like Puerto Vallarta and San Pancho.

- **Taxis:** Taxis are easily accessible in Sayulita and provide a convenient method of transportation for short distances or day trips. Confirm fares before departing, as some taxis may not use meters.

Taxis and Car Rentals

Car rentals and taxis are alternative mobility options in Sayulita for travelers seeking more freedom and autonomy in their exploration.

Car Rental Tips:

- **Renting a Car:** Sayulita car rental firms provide a variety of automobiles to fit a variety of vacation needs. Renting a car allows you to explore the nearby areas and beaches at your leisure.

- **Driving in Sayulita:** The town's roadways can be small and twisting, with limited parking.

Familiarize yourself with local traffic laws and drive with prudence.

Taxi Tips:

- **Availability:** Taxis are available in the town center and can be hailed on the street or found at designated taxi stands.

- **Negotiating Fares:** While some taxis employ meters, it is best to confirm the fare with the driver before beginning your journey, especially if you are traveling a long distance.

Conclusion

Having basic travel tips on hand assures a pleasant and comfortable stay in Sayulita. These recommendations establish the framework for a wonderful vacation on Mexico's Pacific coast, from managing your budget to prioritizing health and safety, knowing local customs, and navigating transportation options. These important travel advices will serve as a dependable guide for a fulfilling and rewarding journey as you explore the bustling streets, relax on the sun-soaked beaches, and immerse yourself in the cultural tapestry of Sayulita.

Chapter 4

ACTIVITIES AND ATTRACTIONS

Exploring Sayulita's activities and attractions is a voyage into a world of sun-kissed beaches, lively cultural experiences, and hidden gems just waiting to be discovered. This chapter delves into Sayulita's coastal beauties, highlighting the pristine beaches, each with its own distinct charm and character.

Sayulita Beaches

Sayulita's coastline is dotted with beaches, each with its own distinct mood and range of activities. Sayulita's beaches are a key component of its attraction, from the vibrant Playa Sayulita to the calm Playa de los Muertos.

Playa Sayulita

The major beach, Playa Sayulita, is the pulsing heart of the town's coastal expanse. The renowned Sayulita sign and the bustling town center frame this lively length of golden sand. Playa Sayulita captures the soul of the town, with surfers riding the waves, beachgoers soaking up the rays, and the dynamic energy of the community reverberating.

Key Features:

- **Surfing Paradise:** Playa Sayulita is well-known for its consistent waves, making it a hotspot for all types of surfers. Whether you're a seasoned surfer or a beginner looking to catch your first wave, the beach is an ideal location for a surfing journey.

- **Beachfront Cafés and Bars:** Beachfront cafés and bars dot the perimeter of Playa Sayulita, providing the ideal environment to drink a refreshing beverage, sample local cuisine, and absorb in the beach atmosphere.

- **Sunbathing & Relaxation**: The broad sandy coastlines beckon visitors to spread out a beach blanket, soak up the rays, and listen to the rhythmic sounds of the Pacific surf.

Activities:

- **Surf Lessons:** There are numerous surf schools near Playa Sayulita that provide lessons for both beginners and advanced surfers. Accept the surf culture and ride the waves with the help of professional instructors.

- **Beach Volleyball:** Play beach volleyball with locals and other travelers. The seaside courts are a hotspot for friendly competition and socializing.

- **Sunset Strolls:** As the day draws to a close, take a leisurely stroll down the shoreline to view the spectacular Sayulita sunsets, which paint the sky in orange and pink hues.

Recommended Beachfront establishments:

Don Pedros Restaurant & Bar: Located directly on the beach, Don Pedros provides an ideal vantage point for watching the surf and sunsets, as well as a scrumptious menu with fresh seafood and Mexican cuisine.

Playa de los Muertos

Playa de los Muertos, which translates as "Beach of the Dead," emanates tranquillity and provides a more private respite than the crowded Playa Sayulita. The name comes from a nearby cemetery, which adds a unique and reflected touch to the beach's mood.

Key Features:

- **Secluded Atmosphere:** Playa de los Muertos offers a more tranquil atmosphere, ideal for those seeking a quieter vacation. The rocky coves and pristine waves of the beach add to its solitary appeal.

- **Artistic Elements:** Art installations and sculptures cover the beach, adding to the bohemian attitude that pervades Sayulita. The artistic components enhance the natural beauty of the setting.

- **Swimming and Snorkeling:** Playa de los Muertos' calm seas make it ideal for swimming and snorkeling. In the pure Pacific waters, explore the underwater environment and find colorful marine life.

Activities:

- **Art Exploration:** Take a leisurely stroll around the beach and examine the numerous art installations and sculptures that enhance the beach's aesthetic appeal.

- **Picnics and Relaxation:** Bring a picnic and unwind on Playa de los Muertos' sandy shoreline. The calm ambiance of the beach is great for a day of leisure.

- **Snorkeling Excursions:** Arrange a snorkeling expedition to explore the marine life in the clear waters around the rocky formations. Guided trips are available from local operators for an immersive underwater experience.

Recommended Beachfront Establishments:

Sayulita Beach House: A beachfront boutique hotel near Playa de los Muertos that provides a tranquil vacation with excellent accommodations and accessible beach access.

Hidden Treasures

Sayulita's coastline is teeming with hidden gems, including isolated coves, immaculate stretches of sand, and natural beauties just waiting to be discovered.

Hidden Treasures:

- **Playa Carricitos:** Playa Carricitos is a hidden gem to the north of Sayulita with quiet environment and beautiful surroundings. A short hike leads to the beach, which provides a peaceful escape.

- **Playa Patzcuaro:** Playa Patzcuaro is a pristine beach surrounded by nature, located to the north of Playa Carricitos. Playa Patzcuaro's pristine beauty makes it a choice among those looking for a more isolated vacation.

- **Marietas Islands:** The Marietas Islands are a short boat trip away from Sayulita. These islands, with their secret beaches and diverse marine life, are a must-see for nature lovers and thrill seekers alike.

Exploration tips:

- **Local Guides:** Hire local guides or tour operators who are knowledgeable with the coastline's hidden beauties. They can offer insights while also ensuring a safe and enjoyable exploration.

- **Nature Walks:** Getting to these hidden gems may take a short hike or nature stroll. Wear comfortable shoes and take advantage of the opportunity to connect with nature.

Preservation Note:

Responsible Exploration: When searching for hidden treasures, practice responsible tourism by respecting the environment, adhering to approved pathways, and avoiding any damages to wildlife or natural ecosystems.

Conclusion

Sayulita's beaches are a patchwork of coastal delights, ranging from the vibrant Playa Sayulita to the tranquil Playa de los Muertos and hidden gems along the coastline.

Whether it's the vibrant surf culture, artistic aspects, or the calm of secluded coves, each beach offers a distinct experience. As you explore these sandy beaches and hidden beauties, you'll realize that Sayulita's beaches are more than just scenery; they're colorful representations of the town's culture.

Water Activities

Sayulita's magnificent Pacific shoreline allows water enthusiasts to immerse themselves in a world of aquatic adventures. Sayulita has a broad choice of water sports to suit any taste, whether you're a seasoned surfer, a snorkeling enthusiast, or someone looking for the thrill of a fishing adventure.

Surfing Spots

Sayulita - A Surfer's Paradise:

Sayulita has established a reputation as a surfer's paradise, attracting surfers from all over the world. Surfers of all ability levels will enjoy the town's steady waves, mild seas, and laid-back environment.

- **Playa Sayulita:**

The town's surf culture is centered on the major beach, Playa Sayulita. Beginner surfers can catch modest waves close to the coast, while more experienced surfers can travel further out for heavier swells. The beach is surrounded with surf schools and rental shops that offer all of the essential equipment as well as skilled assistance to those wishing to ride the waves.

- **Sayulita Point:**

Sayulita Point provides powerful and fast-breaking waves for skilled surfers looking for a challenge. This location is well-known for its steady surf and is popular among surfers wishing to refine their skills on more difficult waves. Sayulita Point's allure is enhanced by the backdrop of beautiful green hills and the famed Sayulita shoreline.

- **La Lancha:**

La Lancha, a short drive or boat trip from Sayulita, is another well-known surf destination. La Lancha is popular among skilled surfers trying to ride the more difficult breaks due to its long, sandy beach and big waves. The beach is surrounded by lush jungle, making for an idyllic location for a day of surfing.

Surfing Advice:

- **Take a Lesson:** If you're new to surfing, try enrolling at one of Sayulita's many surf schools. Experienced teachers can offer valuable advice on technique, safety, and wave reading.

- **Respect Local Rules**: Be cognizant of local surf etiquette, such as right of way on waves and lineup respect. Being respectful in the water guarantees that everyone has a good time.

- **Check the Wave Conditions**: Because surf conditions might change, check the surf forecast before venturing out. Knowing the wave conditions helps you choose the best spot for your ability level, whether you're a beginner or an accomplished surfer.

Diving and Snorkeling

Underwater Wonders of Sayulita:

Beyond the waves, Sayulita has stunning snorkeling and diving chances. The Pacific's crystal-clear waters offer a rich undersea world teeming with marine life, coral reefs, and hidden treasures.

- **Islas Marietas:**

A short boat journey from Sayulita will take you to the famous Islas Marietas, a marine reserve. These islands have crystal-clear waters, bright coral reefs, and a plethora of aquatic life. Snorkelers can explore the underwater caverns and tunnels, where they will see colorful fish, rays, and perhaps a marine turtle.

- **Los Arcos:**

Los Arcos, located south of Sayulita, is another renowned snorkeling and diving destination. These unusual rock formations emerge from the sea, providing an underwater sanctuary for aquatic life. Snorkelers can float past schools of fish, while divers can delve deeper into the ocean to discover secret nooks and crannies.

Snorkeling Tips:

- **Use Eco-Friendly Sunscreen:** When snorkeling, apply reef-safe and eco-friendly sunscreen to safeguard the delicate marine habitat.

Traditional sunscreens have been shown to affect coral reefs and marine life.

- **Respect Marine Life**: Keep a respectful distance from marine life and avoid touching or harming coral reefs. Seeing undersea critters in their natural environment adds to the experience and helps with marine conservation efforts.

- **Guided Tours**: If you're new with the area, consider joining a guided snorkeling tour. Local guides can provide you information about the marine species, assure your safety, and transport you to the best snorkeling sites.

Fishing Excursions

Cast a Line into the Pacific:

Sayulita provides fishing excursions for those who enjoy not only the thrill of the catch but also the opportunity to see the beauty of the Pacific from a fresh perspective.

- **Deep-sea fishing:**

Sayulita's proximity to the Pacific Ocean makes it an ideal starting point for deep-sea fishing excursions. Venture out into the broad waters aboard a hired fishing boat, where you may catch marlin, tuna, dorado, and sailfish. Experienced local captains know the best fishing spots and can lead both novice and experienced anglers.

- **Fishing in estuaries:**

Explore the neighboring estuaries and rivers for a more relaxed fishing experience. Snook, snapper, and tarpon can be found in these calm waters. Estuary fishing has a unique atmosphere, surrounded by lush mangroves and the sounds of nature.

Philosophy of Catch-and-Release:

- **Sustainable Practices:** To safeguard the survival of marine life, many fishing charters in Sayulita follow a catch-and-release attitude. Participate in responsible fishing, and if you decide to keep a catch, make sure it complies with local legislation and sustainable fishing techniques.

- **Local Insights:** Work with local fishing guides to learn about the finest fishing areas, local techniques, and seasonal fluctuations of various fish species. Local knowledge improves the fishing experience and helps to ensure sustainable methods.

Conclusion

Sayulita's aquatic playground encourages visitors to immerse themselves in a world of water activities, from riding the waves at renowned surf areas to snorkeling among vivid coral reefs. Sayulita's numerous water activities cater to all inclinations, whether you're a thrill-seeking surfer, an undersea adventurer, or someone who loves the peacefulness of a fishing vacation.

These activities become more than just experiences as you traverse the Pacific waves and appreciate Sayulita's coastal charm. They become a celebration of the natural beauties that distinguish this Mexican coastal treasure.

Nature and Hiking Trails

Sayulita's lush green hills and beautiful nature trails reveal a new kind of beauty beyond the sun-drenched beaches and blue waters. Hiking and nature paths offer an opportunity to discover the rich biodiversity and stunning landscapes that surround this Mexican seaside town for those looking for a more terrestrial adventure.

Sayulita Ecological Reserve

An Oasis of Biodiversity:

The Sayulita Ecological Reserve exemplifies the town's dedication to protecting its natural assets. This protected region comprises a variety of ecosystems, from tropical forests to riverbeds, giving nature enthusiasts and hikers with an immersive experience.

Trail Overview:

The reserve has well-kept trails that weave through lush foliage, providing glimpses of native flora and fauna. Hiking through the Sayulita Ecological Reserve is a peaceful respite from the town core, immersing visitors in the sights and sounds of nature.

Fauna and Flora:

As you walk the paths, you'll come across a number of indigenous plant and animal species. A symphony of nature is created by towering trees, bright wildflowers, and the musical songs of tropical birds. Iguanas, butterflies, and rare bird species can all be found in the reserve.

Scenic vistas:

The pathways lead to elevated viewpoints with panoramic views of Sayulita and its surroundings. Take in the fresh air while gazing out at the Pacific Ocean, the town's red-tiled roofs, and the verdant hills that surround Sayulita. These gorgeous vistas are ideal for wildlife enthusiasts and photographers.

Hiking Advice:

- **Guided Tours:** Join a guided hiking tour to learn about the reserve's flora and fauna. Knowledgeable guides can give knowledge about the area's biological importance and improve your overall hiking experience.

- **Bring the essentials:** Bring water, sunscreen, and good hiking shoes. Because the tropical temperature can be hot, staying hydrated is critical. It is also advisable to wear a helmet and use insect repellent.

Monkey Mountain Trail

A Relaxing Jungle Trek:

The Monkey Mountain Trail is a mesmerizing adventure through the jungle that leads hikers to a top with spectacular views of the Pacific shoreline. This trail is popular with those looking for a more difficult hike with the added bonus of encountering wildlife.

Highlights of the Trail:

The Monkey Mountain Trail starts in the beautiful foliage that surrounds Sayulita and progressively ascends, offering views of the town and its surroundings. The trail is named by the presence of howler monkeys, which can be seen hanging across the treetops on occasion.

Wildlife Encounters:

Keep a look out for the various species that makes Monkey Mountain home as you walk the trail. Along with howler monkeys, you might see tropical birds, butterflies, and even the elusive coatimundi. The natural surroundings of the trail create a serene ambiance, allowing hikers to connect with the nature.

Panoramic Summit Views:

The Monkey Mountain Trail culminates at the peak, where hikers are rewarded with panoramic views stretching from the ocean to the inland hills. The vantage point provides a wonderful opportunity to explore Sayulita's various sceneries.

Hiking Advice:

- **Sturdy Footwear:** Because the Monkey Mountain Trail includes uneven terrain, wearing sturdy hiking shoes with good traction is necessary. The ascent can be steep in places, therefore wearing appropriate footwear is recommended.

- **Early Morning climb:** To avoid the noon heat, consider starting your climb early in the morning. The milder temperatures not only make the trek more enjoyable, but they also boost the chances of seeing wildlife.

Conclusion

Hiking paths in Sayulita offer visitors to discover the town's natural attractions beyond its famed beaches. From the tranquil trails of the Sayulita Ecological Reserve to the more difficult ascent of Monkey Mountain, these treks provide opportunities to interact with nature, witness varied ecosystems, and enjoy panoramic views of the Pacific coastline.

Sayulita's hiking and outdoor experiences become a journey of discovery as you walk the well-trodden paths or venture into the less-explored trails, gaining a greater appreciation of the town's ecological richness and the importance of maintaining its natural legacy.

Cultural Experiences

Sayulita's vibrant ambiance and rich cultural tapestry entice tourists to immerse themselves in a world of artistic expression, local markets bursting with craftsmanship, and colorful events that highlight the town's dynamic personality. This chapter delves into the cultural experiences that make Sayulita a creative and celebratory hotspot.

Art Galleries

Display of Creative Expression:

Sayulita's artistic essence is on full display in its diverse art galleries, each offering a unique perspective on the creativity and talent blossoming in this coastal town.

Galería Tanana:

Galería Tanana is a well-known exhibitor of modern Mexican art. The gallery exhibits works by emerging and known artists in a variety of mediums ranging from paintings and sculptures to mixed-media installations. Visitors can explore the curated displays that embody the essence of Mexican culture as well as Sayulita's varied spirit.

Community Space for Entreamigos:

Entreamigos is a community place that promotes creativity and ecological living, rather than a traditional art gallery. The location hosts art workshops, exhibitions, and installations, allowing local artists and artisans to showcase their skills. Visitors can participate in seminars or simply stroll around the evolving art pieces that reflect the community's dedication to innovation and collaboration.

La Hamaca:

La Hamaca is an art gallery in Sayulita that emphasizes the combination of traditional and contemporary Mexican art. The gallery exhibits paintings, fabrics, and handcrafted artifacts that express the essence of Mexican culture. La Hamaca's devotion to local artists guarantees that each piece tells a narrative and adds to Sayulita's lively artistic scene.

Art Gallery Tips:

- **Gallery Walks:** Because of Sayulita's narrow layout, gallery walks are popular. Take a leisurely stroll across town, stopping at several galleries along the way.

- **Meet the Artists:** Many galleries in Sayulita have on-site artists or curators who are eager to share insights on the pieces on display. Don't be afraid to strike up a discussion to learn more about the creative process.

Local Markets

Sayulita Market Treasures:

The local markets in Sayulita are a treasure mine of handmade items, traditional relics, and the vivid spirit of local artisans. These markets give a look into the town's cultural past as well as the opportunity to purchase one-of-a-kind souvenirs.

Sayulita Mercado del Pueblo:

The Sayulita Mercado del Pueblo, held every Friday, is a crowded farmers' market that transforms the town center into a frenetic hub of activity. Local vendors set up stalls selling fresh food, handmade jewelry, and organic delights. The market not only supports local farmers and artists, but it also serves as a bustling community gathering place for residents and visitors alike.

Tianguis Lo de Marcos:

Although not in Sayulita, the Tianguis (weekly market) at adjacent Lo de Marcos is worth a visit. This traditional market features handwoven fabrics, pottery, and indigenous items made by local artisans. The Tianguis provides a cultural immersion into the neighboring region of Sayulita.

Feria Tianguis Cultural:

The Feria Tianguis Cultural is a cultural market that takes place on a regular basis and features a wide range of handmade products, artwork, and live performances.

Sayulita's commitment to fostering cultural interaction and nurturing local talent is exemplified by this market.

Market Tips:

- **Support Local Artisans:** Prioritize products manufactured by local craftspeople when purchasing at local marketplaces. These items frequently have a distinct cultural value and directly contribute to the community's livelihood.

- **Engage with Vendors:** Take advantage of the opportunity to speak with the vendors. Many of them are enthusiastic about their work and are eager to tell you about it.

Festivals and Events

Lively Celebrations in Sayulita:

Sayulita's calendar is jam-packed with festivals and events honoring the town's cultural diversity, artistic expression, and lively community spirit. Attending these events delivers an immersive glimpse into Sayulita's lively culture.

Sayulita Festival de Arte:

The annual Sayulita Festival de Arte celebrates the visual and performing arts. The town is transformed into an open-air gallery, displaying works by local and international artists. During this bustling festival, visitors can explore art installations, witness live performances, and engage with the creative energy that pervades the streets.

Día de los Muertos (Day of the Dead):

Sayulita's Da de los Muertos event is a moving and colorful ode to Mexican traditions. The town comes alive with colorful altars, parades, and memorial services for dead loved ones. Visitors can see the beautiful papel picado decorations, consume traditional meals, and join in the community celebration of life and death.

Film Festival in Sayulita:

Filmmakers, artists, and cinephiles from all over the world attend the Sayulita Film Festival. This yearly festival features a carefully curated variety of indie films, documentaries, and short films. Aside from screenings, the festival features panel discussions, workshops, and opportunities to connect with filmmakers, resulting in a vibrant forum for cultural interaction.

Event Tips:

- Check the town's event calendar before organizing your trip to coincide with festivals or events that interest you.

- **Involve Yourself:** Attend classes, interact with artists, and immerse yourself in the cultural offerings to actively participate in the festivities.

Conclusion

Beyond its natural beauty and outdoor activities, Sayulita's cultural experiences invite tourists to explore the town's creative soul and active personality. Sayulita offers a full cultural immersion, with art galleries showcasing contemporary Mexican art, local markets packed with homemade treasures, and bustling festivals celebrating the diversity of Mexican culture.

As you walk through the bright streets, interact with local craftsmen, and take part in the town's festivities, you'll realize that Sayulita's cultural experiences are more than just activities; they're windows into the heart and soul of this wonderful coastal town.

Chapter 5

DINING AND CULINARY DELIGHTS

The gastronomic scene of Sayulita is a lively tapestry of tastes, a blend of traditional Mexican cuisine and new culinary inventions. This chapter is a culinary tour through Sayulita's eclectic dining scene, relishing popular local dishes and indulging in the seafood delicacies, street food, and classic Mexican meals that make the town a foodie heaven.

Culinary Scene in Sayulita

An Eclectic Culinary Paradise:

The food scene in Sayulita reflects the town's diversified and dynamic atmosphere. The streets are crowded with restaurants ranging from simple taco vendors to sophisticated restaurants, each having its own touch on Mexican and international food. The town's attention to freshness and quality ingredients, which are frequently acquired locally, elevates the eating experience to a flavor fiesta.

Ambience and Diversity:

Sayulita's dining establishments not only offer a variety of culinary influences, but also a variety of atmospheres. From coastal palapas where you may dine with your toes in the sand to bustling taco shops in the town center, the selections cater to a wide range of tastes, making eating an immersive and unforgettable experience.

Commitment to Farm-to-Table:

Many Sayulita restaurants follow a farm-to-table philosophy, sourcing fresh produce, seafood, and meats from local farmers and fishermen. This dedication to sustainability not only improves the quality of the food, but also contributes to the town's overall attitude of supporting local companies and decreasing environmental impact.

Popular local Dishes

Sayulita's Characteristic Flavors:

To properly comprehend Sayulita's culinary essence, one must delve into the town's popular local dishes, which represent the town's seaside location, rich cultural background, and enjoyment of bold, colorful flavors. Sayulita's gastronomy offers a delicious choice of options for every palate, from seafood specialties to street food delights and classic Mexican cuisine.

Seafood Specialties

- **The Pacific's Bounty**:

Sayulita's beachfront location along the Pacific Ocean results in an abundance of seafood that graces many menus. The seafood specialties embody the essence of the town's marine past, from ceviche to grilled fish tacos.

- **Ceviche de Pescado**:

Ceviche, a refreshing and tangy dish, is a Sayulita classic. Fresh fish marinated in lime juice with diced tomatoes, onions, cilantro, and chili peppers, generally marlin, snapper, or shrimp.

As a result, the zesty flavors enhance the succulence of the seafood. Ceviche, whether served as a simple appetizer or as a main course, represents the town's commitment to fresh, local ingredients.

- **Fish Tacos:**

Sayulita's fish tacos are a gourmet treat not to be missed. The fish of the day, grilled or battered, is wrapped in a warm corn tortilla and topped with shredded cabbage, pico de gallo, and a drizzle of creamy sauce. A classic coastal eating experience is created by the blend of crispy textures and vivid flavors.

- **Mariscada:**

Mariscada is the answer for those looking for a seafood frenzy. In a thick tomato-based broth, this substantial seafood stew offers an assortment of ocean treasures such as shrimp, octopus, mussels, and fish. Mariscada is a savory and rich dish that shows the depth of Pacific flavors when served with rice or crusty bread.

Street Food

- **Flavors on the Go:**

The aromas of street cuisine fill the streets of Sayulita, offering a variety of quick eats and savory snacks.

Street food sellers, typically nestled into lively corners of town, offer a culinary excursion for anyone looking to sample real Mexican flavors.

- **Tacos al Pastor:**

Tacos al pastor, a traditional street food staple, are a must-try in Sayulita. Thin slices of marinated pork are stacked vertically on a rotisserie, similar to shawarma, and then finely shaved onto a corn tortilla. Tacos al pastor have a fantastic blend of salty and sweet flavors when topped with pineapple, onions, cilantro, and salsa.

- **Elote:**

Elote is a popular Mexican street snack that consists of grilled corn on the cob that has been coated with mayonnaise, dusted with chili powder, and served with lime juice and cotija cheese. As a result, the elote becomes a symphony of smokey, spicy, and sour tastes, making it a popular and enjoyable street food.

- **Tamales:**

Tamales are also available on the streets of Sayulita. These steamed packages of masa dough are wrapped in corn husks and stuffed with various items such as meats, chiles, and veggies. Tamales highlight the richness of Mexican cuisine, and street vendors frequently offer a variety of flavors to tempt your taste buds.

Traditional Mexican cuisine

- **Rooted in Culinary Heritage:**

Sayulita's culinary journey includes traditional Mexican cuisine, which honors time-honored traditions and culinary skills. Exploring traditional Mexican cuisine, from creamy moles to savory enchiladas, provides a fuller appreciation of the country's gastronomic legacy.

- **Mole Poblano:**

Mole, a thick and rich sauce, is revered in Mexican cuisine. Mole Poblano, from the Mexican state of Puebla, is a dark, velvety sauce prepared with chilies, chocolate, spices, and sometimes nuts. The end result is a taste symphony that goes beautifully with meats, particularly chicken. Restaurants in Sayulita that specialize in traditional Mexican cuisine frequently include mole dishes on their menus.

- **Enchiladas Suiza:**

Enchiladas Suizas are a traditional Mexican comfort food that combines Mexican and Swiss culinary elements. Corn tortillas are stuffed with shredded chicken and rolled before being topped with a creamy tomatillo salsa and melted cheese. The name "Suizas" relates to the dish's Swiss-style creaminess, which creates a delectable balance of textures and flavors.

- **Tacos de Carnitas:**

Carnitas, or slow-cooked and seasoned pork, are a typical Mexican dish. Tacos de Carnitas highlight the dish's juicy and savory quality. Slow cooking yields delicate, juicy pork that is frequently served with sliced onions, cilantro, and a touch of lime. Tacos de Carnitas demonstrate the creativity of traditional Mexican cooking methods.

Dining tips:

Local Markets: For a true gastronomic experience, visit local markets and try a range of street cuisine and traditional specialties.

Request Recommendations: Locals are frequently the most knowledgeable about undiscovered culinary gems. Don't be afraid to seek advice from locals or fellow visitors.

Embrace Mealtimes: Meals are a social event in Mexico, and adopting the culture of unhurried dining helps you to taste the flavors and immerse yourself in the gastronomic experience.

Conclusion

Sayulita's dining scene is a gastronomic adventure that allows you to sample Pacific flavors, indulge in street food pleasures, and discover the complexity of traditional Mexican cuisine.

Dining in Sayulita is more than a necessity; it's a celebration of culture, community, and the vibrant spirit that defines this enchanting coastal town, from the seafood specialties that celebrate the town's coastal bounty to the lively street food offerings and the rich tapestry of traditional Mexican dishes. You'll discover that each mouthful is a trip into the heart of Sayulita's rich gastronomic legacy as you explore the various culinary environment.

Cafes and Restaurants

Sayulita's culinary scene goes beyond street food and traditional Mexican fare, offering a varied range of dining experiences to suit a variety of tastes and budgets. This chapter delves into the range of dining alternatives in Sayulita, from fine dining facilities that enrich the gourmet experience to budget-friendly eateries and those that cater to vegan and vegetarian preferences.

Options for Fine Dining

Elevating the Culinary Experience:

Sayulita's fine dining options highlight the town's gastronomic growth, blending great flavors, imaginative presentations, and, on occasion, spectacular views. These restaurants offer a refined dining experience, inviting guests to appreciate the craftsmanship of chefs who draw inspiration from both local foods and international culinary trends.

- **Don Pedro's:**

Don Pedro's is a famous fine dining institution in Sayulita, located on the seaside with breathtaking views of the Pacific Ocean. The restaurant has a classy environment as well as a broad menu that includes fresh seafood, top cuts of meat, and creative cocktails.

The romantic atmosphere created by the al fresco eating area, embellished with glittering lights, makes it a great choice for a special evening.

- **Tequila Lounge and Mejico Grill:**

Mejico Grill and Tequila Lounge serve contemporary Mexican food with a contemporary touch. The restaurant has a sophisticated atmosphere and a large range of tequila. The dishes are expertly created, mixing traditional Mexican flavors with cutting-edge culinary techniques. The cuisine of Mejico Grill displays the richness of Mexican gastronomy, with dishes ranging from ceviche to mole.

- **Sayulita's Beach Café:**

Sayulita Café on the Beach offers a unique environment right on Playa Sayulita for exquisite dining with your toes in the sand. The restaurant's menu emphasizes locally produced products, resulting in meals that highlight the region's freshness and richness. Diners can experience a fantastic culinary journey by the sea with the sound of waves in the background.

Tips for Fine Dining:

- **Reservations:** Fine dining restaurants in Sayulita can be crowded, especially during high seasons. To guarantee a table, make reservations in advance, especially if you have a specific date or time in mind.

- **Dress Code:** There may be a dress code at some fine dining establishments. While Sayulita has a relaxed attitude in general, it's a good idea to verify the restaurant's dress code and dress properly for a more comfortable eating experience.

Budget-Friendly Restaurants

Flavor on a Shoestring:

Sayulita realizes that not every delectable dining experience necessitates a high price. The area is studded with budget-friendly restaurants that deliver tasty, filling meals without sacrificing flavor. These restaurants offer a taste of Sayulita's culinary delights while keeping varied economic restraints in mind.

- **ChocoBanana:**

ChocoBanana is a well-known Sayulita institution that has been feeding locals and guests for many years. ChocoBanana offers a casual and laid-back ambiance and is known for its hearty breakfasts, fresh fruit smoothies, and a range of Mexican and foreign entrees. ChocoBanana is a budget-friendly solution whether you're starting your day with a traditional Mexican breakfast or grabbing a quick snack.

- **El Itacate:**

El Itacate is a popular alternative for people looking for authentic Mexican street food at a reasonable price. This laid-back restaurant serves tacos, quesadillas, and tortas stuffed with tasty meats and traditional garnishes. El Itacate is a go-to destination for a great supper without breaking the bank thanks to its simple menu and speedy service.

- **La Rustica:**

La Rustica is a cozy pizzeria that serves affordable Italian cuisine. The menu contains classic favorites created with high-quality ingredients, ranging from wood-fired pizzas to pasta dishes. The relaxing atmosphere and outdoor seats make La Rustica an excellent alternative for those looking for a simple and economical dining experience.

Budget-Friendly Suggestions:

- **Explore Street cuisine:** Sayulita's streets are teeming with vendors selling cheap and tasty street cuisine. Tacos, elote, and tamales from street sellers offer a taste of the local delicacies at reasonable costs.

- **Daily Specials:** Many Sayulita restaurants, especially those with fine dining ambitions, offer daily specials or prix-fixe meals that are less expensive than ordering à la carte. To get the most of your dining budget, look for daily offers.

Vegetarian and Vegan Options

Plant-Based Culinary Delights:

Sayulita caters to vegans and vegetarians with a variety of restaurants that emphasize the availability of fresh vegetables and inventive plant-based cookery. These restaurants highlight Sayulita's vegan and vegetarian cuisine's innovation and flexibility.

- **The Real Coconut:**

The Real Coconut, located on the lovely grounds of Haramara Retreat, is a plant-based restaurant that promotes clean and organic cuisine. The menu includes vegan and gluten-free options ranging from healthy bowls and tacos to smoothie bowls and desserts. The Real Coconut's commitment to sustainability extends beyond its culinary offerings, making it a popular choice for people looking for mindful and plant-based dining.

- **La Esperanza:**

La Esperanza is a vegetarian and vegan-friendly restaurant that accommodates a wide range of dietary needs. Vegetarian tacos, plant-based burgers, and inventive salads created with locally sourced ingredients are on the menu. Sayulita's culinary versatility is enhanced by the restaurant's focus to providing savory and fulfilling plant-based options.

- **Revolución del Sueño:**

Revolución del Sueo is a vegetarian and vegan restaurant recognized for its innovative menu and lively ambiance. The menu features a combination of flavors that appeal to a wide range of preferences, from plant-based burritos to vegan sushi rolls. The restaurant's commitment to sustainability and community engagement is consistent with Sayulita's concept.

Tips for Vegans and Vegetarians:

- **Explore Local Ingredients:** Because Sayulita places an emphasis on fresh, local goods, it is simple to find delicious and nutritious vegan and vegetarian options. Investigate meals that showcase regional cuisines.

- **Customization:** Many Sayulita restaurants are willing to accommodate special requests. To accommodate your dietary needs, feel free to request vegan or vegetarian adjustments to current menu items.

Conclusion

The dining scene in Sayulita is a kaleidoscope of cuisines that cater to a wide range of tastes, preferences, and budgets.

Sayulita's culinary scene is a tribute to the town's vibrant and welcoming attitude, whether you're enjoying in fine dining with breathtaking ocean views, relishing budget-friendly street food, or discovering the inventive and diverse options of vegan and vegetarian establishments.

Each meal becomes an opportunity to discover the unique blend of culinary traditions, innovative twists, and the vibrant community that defines Sayulita's gastronomic identity as you navigate the diverse dining establishments.

Chapter 6

NIGHTLIFE AND ENTERTAINMENT

The appeal of Sayulita does not wane with the setting sun; rather, the town comes alive with a dynamic nightlife that reflects its vivacious and varied personality.

After dark, Chapter 6 digs into the pulsating core of Sayulita, examining its bars and nightclubs, seaside venues, live music scenes, and the variety of evening entertainment options that make the town a lively nightlife hub.

Nightclubs and Bars

Where the Nights Come Alive:

The nightlife in Sayulita is a celebration of music, laughing, and the companionship that thrives under the starlit sky. The town's bars and nightclubs appeal to a wide range of preferences, offering everything from coastal calm to lively dance floors where locals and visitors alike can delight in the beat of the night.

Beachfront bars

Sipping by the Shore:

The beachfront bars in Sayulita are lovely havens where the Pacific breeze mingles with patrons' laughter. These restaurants offer a relaxed and scenic setting, inviting customers to unwind with a glass in hand and the soothing sound of waves as a backdrop.

- **Don Pato's:**

Don Pato's, located along the beach, offers a relaxing and rustic setting that embodies Sayulita's seaside appeal. Don Pato's offers a beachfront experience that perfectly merges calm with the boisterous energy of Sayulita's nightlife, whether you're enjoying a margarita while watching the sunset or joining the evening crowd for live music.

- **Sayulita Beach Club:**

The Sayulita Beach Club offers an attractive location with spectacular ocean views for those looking for a more upmarket beachside experience. Enjoy the ambient music or DJ sounds that create a classy yet laid-back ambiance while sipping a cocktail and dipping your toes in the sand. The beach club frequently hosts special events, making each visit a one-of-a-kind experience.

Beachfront Bar tips:

- **Sunset Sessions:** Many seaside establishments host special sunset sessions that include live music or DJ sets. Arrive early to have an excellent view of the spectacular sunset over the Pacific.

- For a more pleasant experience, consider wearing sandals or beach-appropriate footwear given the sandy terrain.

Venues for Live Music

Rhythmic nights:

The live music venues in Sayulita are the throbbing core of the town's nightlife, giving a platform for both local and international performers to showcase their talents. From quiet concerts to high-energy shows, Sayulita's live music culture ensures that nights are filled with rhythm and melody.

- **Escondido Sports Bar:**

Escondido Sports Bar is a dynamic establishment that serves not only to sports fans but also evolves into a vibrant live music venue in the nights. Escondido is home to a diverse range of musical groups, from rock bands to acoustic duos. The warm atmosphere and numerous music options make it a local and visiting favorite.

- **Sayulita Public House:**

Sayulita Public House mixes the intensity of a live music venue with the ambiance of a bar. This small venue frequently hosts local bands, solo performers, and themed music nights. The Public House's dedication to promoting a sense of community is reflected in its diversified music offering, which appeals to Sayulita's diverse clientele.

Live Music Venue tips:

- **Examine Event Calendars:** Many live music venues have event calendars or social media accounts where forthcoming performances are announced. Check out these tools to arrange your night around live music events that match your musical tastes.

- **Diverse genres:** Sayulita's live music scene includes a wide range of genres, from traditional Mexican music to rock, reggae, and electronic beats. Explore various venues to get a sense of the breadth of musical offerings.

Evening Entertainment

Diverse Delights After Dark:

Sayulita's nighttime entertainment alternatives are a testament to the town's commitment to providing various and fascinating activities for night owls, beyond the sounds of live music and the ambiance of seaside pubs. Sayulita's evenings are as varied as they are enchanting, with everything from outdoor movie nights beneath the stars to cultural acts that highlight the variety of Mexican customs.

Outdoor Movie Nights

The Sky Over Sayulita:

Sayulita's wide areas are transformed into cinematic experiences under the stars during outdoor movie nights. These events, which are frequently hosted by local businesses, offer a unique and relaxed way to view films while enjoying the coastal breeze and the companionship of other moviegoers.

- ### Movie Nights at Sayulita Plaza:

The Sayulita Plaza, located in the heart of town, organizes outdoor movie nights that attract both locals and visitors. The open-air location lets attendees to bring blankets or beach chairs, creating a warm and social movie-watching experience for classic and modern releases.

Hotel Cinco Movie Nights:

Hotel Cinco, a boutique hotel in Sayulita, organizes movie nights by the pool on occasion. This experience blends luxury with the charm of outdoor theater, thanks to the serene settings and the shimmering water reflecting the movie on a giant screen.

Outdoor Movie Night tips:

- **Blankets & Comfort:** While many outdoor movie nights include seating, bringing a blanket or beach chair adds to the experience. Evenings can be cooler than predicted due to the coastal breeze.

- **Schedules should be checked:** Outdoor movie evenings may not be a regular occurrence, so check with nearby venues, hotels, or community boards for upcoming events.

Cultural Displays

Celebrating Tradition:

The variety of cultural performances that take place in the evenings demonstrates Sayulita's commitment to conserving and sharing its cultural legacy. These performances, which range from traditional dances to theatrical plays, provide an insight into the richness of Mexican cultures.

Plaza Cultural Performances:

The Sayulita Plaza, a popular gathering place, features cultural performances that feature traditional Mexican dances, music, and folklore on occasion. These events highlight the town's cultural diversity and provide a venue for local entertainers to showcase their abilities to the community.

Community Space for Entreamigos:

Entreamigos, a Sayulita community center, is dedicated to promoting education, creativity, and cultural exchange. Cultural acts such as theatrical shows, dance recitals, and music concerts are frequently held in the venue. These activities add to Sayulita's diverse cultural tapestry and give a venue for artistic expression.

Cultural Performance tips:

- **Interact with the Performers:** Cultural performances frequently include audience engagement. Engage with the performances, ask questions, and immerse yourself in the cultural experience.

- **Support Community spaces:** Many cultural acts are held in community venues that rely on the generosity of residents and tourists. Consider giving a donation or getting involved in community projects to help preserve cultural practices.

Calendar of Local Events

Keeping Up to Date:

Sayulita's vibrant nightlife and evening entertainment are frequently supplemented by special events and festivals that occur throughout the year. Keeping track of the events schedule allows you to plan your visit around unique and unforgettable activities, from local celebrations to worldwide meetings.

Sayulita Festivals & Events:

Throughout the year, the town holds a variety of events and festivals, including the Sayulita Film Festival and the Sayulita Festival de Arte. These gatherings bring locals and visitors together, creating a dynamic atmosphere that goes beyond the traditional nightlife scene. Checking the local events schedule guarantees that you don't miss out on any exciting events during your visit.

Weekly Events:

In Sayulita, certain days of the week have become associated with distinct events. Keeping an eye on the weekly events schedule allows you to personalize your evenings to your interests, from live music nights to themed parties. Many places post the week's lineup on their social media profiles or chalkboards.

Event Calendar tips:

- **Local Recommendations:** Locals frequently have insider information on future events and festivals. Start talks with locals or ask for recommendations at nearby businesses.

- **Plan Ahead:** If you have a particular event or festival in mind, schedule your visit accordingly. Because some events draw enormous crowds, it is best to book accommodations and transportation ahead of time.

Conclusion

The nightlife and evening activities in Sayulita are dynamic manifestations of the town's vivid personality. Each evening in Sayulita becomes a new and beautiful experience, whether you're sipping cocktails at a seaside bar, swaying to live music beneath the stars, experiencing an outdoor movie night, immersing yourself in cultural activities, or matching your stay with local events.

The sense of community, cultural richness, and sheer joy of celebration create an atmosphere that urges you to dance, laugh, and experience the charm of Sayulita's nightlife as the town comes alive after dark.

Chapter 7

DAY TRIPS AND EXCURSIONS

Sayulita's allure extends beyond its sandy beaches, enticing visitors to explore the neighboring attractions and exhilarating activities that surround this coastal paradise.

Chapter 7 is a day trip and excursion guide, including neighboring sites and adrenaline-pumping adventure tours that allow guests to see the different landscapes and activities that await just beyond Sayulita's borders.

Nearby Destinations

Exploration of the Periphery:

Sayulita is a gateway to a plethora of enthralling destinations that highlight the beauty and diversity of the Nayarit region. Nearby destinations, ranging from quaint coastal villages to pristine islands, provide an opportunity to explore beyond Sayulita's embrace and immerse oneself in new landscapes and cultures.

Punta de Mita

A Luxurious Coastal Escape:

Punta de Mita is a premium destination noted for its upscale resorts, scenic beaches, and world-class golf courses. It is located just south of Sayulita. The town exudes sophistication while keeping a relaxed vibe, making it a great day excursion for those looking for a taste of exquisite coastal living.

Key attractions:

- **Four Seasons Resort Punta Mita:** Indulge in luxury at the Four Seasons Resort, which features excellent accommodations, fine cuisine, and a golf course built by Jack Nicklaus.

- **Playa Punta de Mita:** Unwind on the golden sands of Playa Punta de Mita, a tranquil beach with clean seas ideal for swimming and water sports.

- **Surfing:** Punta de Mita is well-known for its surf breaks, which draw surfers looking for the ideal wave.

Recommendation:

Gourmet Dining: Taste the region's seafood and worldwide tastes at seaside restaurants and upmarket dining selections in Punta de Mita.

San Pancho

Tranquil Vibes and Artistic Charms:

San Pancho (officially San Francisco) is a short drive north of Sayulita and offers a more calm and artistic ambiance. This coastal town has managed to keep its bohemian appeal while also becoming a center for art, culture, and environmentally friendly activities.

Key Attractions:

- **EntreAmigos:** Visit EntreAmigos, a community center that promotes education and sustainability. The facility includes art seminars, cultural activities, and a store selling recycled art.

- **Sayulita Polo Club:** For a one-of-a-kind experience, attend a polo match at the Sayulita Polo Club, which showcases the region's equestrian culture.

- **San Pancho Beach:** Relax and enjoy the laid-back atmosphere of San Pancho Beach, which is noted for its immaculate sands and breathtaking sunsets.

Recommendation:

Explore San Pancho's thriving art scene on a Friday during the weekly Art Walk, when galleries open their doors to present local and international artists.

Marietas Islands

Hidden Natural Wonders:

Take a boat trip to the Marietas Islands, a protected archipelago famed for its diverse marine life and beautiful sceneries. A short boat journey from Sayulita, these islands provide a dreamlike getaway into nature's beauties.

Key Attractions:

- **Hidden Beach:** Visit the famous Hidden Beach, a hidden cove nestled beneath a collapsed volcanic crater. It's a weird and scenic area that may be reached by swimming or kayaking via a cave.

- **Marine Biodiversity:** Snorkel or dive to discover the rich underwater world that surrounds the islands, which is home to colorful coral reefs and a wide range of marine creatures.

- **Bird Watching:** The islands are a birdwatcher's delight, with a wide variety of bird species such as blue-footed boobies and frigatebirds.

Recommendation:

Guided Tours: Because the Marietas Islands are protected, guided tours are required. Snorkeling, kayaking, and bird-watching excursions are available from local tour providers.

Adventure Tours

Exciting Escapades:

Sayulita and its surrounding environs offer a variety of adventure tours that blend natural beauty with heart-pounding activities for those looking for an adrenaline rush. These trips provide an amazing way to experience the region, from soaring over the treetops on zip lines to exploring difficult terrain on ATVs.

Zip-lining Adventures

Canopy Soaring:

The lush surroundings of Sayulita are excellent for zip-lining activities, which allow participants to soar through the treetops while enjoying panoramic views of the jungle and ocean.

Key Experiences:

- **Jungle Canopy Zipline:** Experience the thrill of zip-lining through the jungle canopy, with several platforms and lines providing varied vistas of the terrain.

- **Sunset Zip-lining:** Some operators provide sunset zip-lining adventures, allowing customers to experience the excitement against the backdrop of a vibrant Pacific sunset.

Safety Note:

Choose zip-lining providers who have certified guides and modern equipment to ensure a safe and pleasurable experience.

ATV Tours

Rugged Terrain Exploration:

ATV tours are a challenging and exciting way to see the different landscapes that surround Sayulita. ATV tours, whether through forest trails or along seaside paths, provide a hands-on view of the region's natural beauty.

Key Experiences:

- **Jungle and Beach ATV trips**: Explore the jungle trails and beach paths on guided ATV trips that combine adrenaline and scenic exploration.

- **Private trips**: Some operators provide private ATV trips, which allow for a more personalized experience that is tailored to individual interests.

Environmental Consideration:

To reduce environmental effect, choose ATV operators who are committed to responsible and sustainable methods. To safeguard natural habitats, stay on authorized pathways.

Boat Excursions

Seafaring Adventures:

Sayulita's coastline location makes it a great starting point for boat excursions to experience the beauty of the Pacific Ocean. These boat cruises offer a marine adventure, from whale watching to snorkeling in remote coves.

Key Experiences:

- **Whale Watching:** During the winter months, go whale watching to see the migration of humpback whales. These magnificent marine creatures are well-known in the waters of Sayulita.

- **Snorkeling Tours:** Take a snorkeling trip to discover secret coves and beautiful underwater habitats. Many cruises include stops at scenic locations such as the Marietas Islands.

- **Fishing Charters:** For those who enjoy fishing, hire a boat for a deep-sea experience. The Pacific waters around Sayulita are teeming with marine life, making it possible to catch a variety of fish.

Eco-friendly Practices:

Choose Sustainable Operators: Choose boat operators who are devoted to environmentally beneficial methods, such as responsible wildlife viewing and trash reduction projects.

Conclusion

Sayulita's allure extends beyond its sandy beaches, enticing visitors to explore the different landscapes and experiences that surround this coastal paradise. Day travels to nearby sites such as Punta de Mita, San Pancho, or the Marietas Islands, or adrenaline-pumping thrills on zip lines, ATVs, or boat excursions, each excursion promises to add a new depth to the Sayulita experience.

These day outings and experiences not only highlight the region's natural beauty, but also offer possibilities for cultural immersion and thrilling escapades that complement Sayulita's laid-back appeal.

As you explore Sayulita's outskirts, you'll realize that the enchantment of this seaside paradise stretches far beyond its borders, enticing you to explore, appreciate, and make lasting memories.

Chapter 8

SHOPPING IN SAYULITA

Sayulita's dynamic and eclectic environment extends to its shopping scene, which features a delectable selection of local markets, artisanal boutiques, and unique souvenirs. Chapter 8 is your journey to Sayulita's retail delights, from lively marketplaces to secret boutiques that showcase the town's rich creative and cultural attractions.

Local Markets and Bazaars

Discovering Local Flavors:

Sayulita's local markets and bazaars are vibrant concentrations of activity where the town's colors, noises, and scents collide. These markets offer an unique shopping experience, ranging from fresh vegetables to handcrafted products, and serve as a window into Sayulita's heart.

Sayulita Mercado

A Tapestry of Local wares:

The Sayulita Mercado is the town's pulsing heart, showing the ingenuity and craftsmanship of local artisans and traders. This market, located in the heart of Sayulita, is a vivid mosaic of stalls selling a wide range of things, from handmade jewelry to traditional Mexican dishes.

Key Attractions:

- **Handmade Crafts:** Visit stalls selling locally manufactured goods such as handwoven textiles, pottery, and beautiful beadwork.

- **Fresh Produce:** The market is a treasure trove of tropical fruits, vegetables, and spices.

- **Local Cuisine:** Indulge in typical Mexican street food and snacks offered at numerous vendors, delivering a sample of Sayulita's culinary delicacies.

Shopping Tips:

- **Bargaining:** In Sayulita markets, bargaining is widespread. Polite bargaining can yield favorable results, especially when purchasing many things.

- **Cash is king:** While some vendors take credit cards, it's best to have cash on hand because cash is the preferred mode of payment for many stalls.

Artisan Shops

Hidden Creativity Treasures:

Sayulita is peppered with artisanal businesses showcasing the work of local and regional artists. These stores are havens for anyone looking for one-of-a-kind and handcrafted things ranging from clothing and accessories to home décor and artwork.

Key Attractions:

- **Boutique Clothing:** Look for boutique clothing boutiques that provide a curated variety of bohemian-inspired items, frequently handcrafted by local designers.

- **Art Galleries:** Explore art galleries that showcase a wide range of artworks, such as paintings, sculptures, and mixed-media works by both emerging and recognized artists.

- **Home Décor:** Many artisanal stores specialize in one-of-a-kind home décor products like handwoven rugs, ceramics, and ornate furnishings.

Shopping Tips:

- **Inquire About Artists:** Inquire about the artists who created the works. Many shops have relationships with local artists, and understanding about the story behind the products adds to the value of the products.

- **Options for Customization:** Some handmade establishments provide customization services. Think of personalized things as unique keepsakes or gifts.

Souvenirs and Handcrafted Items

Bringing a Piece of Sayulita Home:

Souvenirs and handicrafts in Sayulita are more than just keepsakes; they are representations of the town's lively culture and artistic character. From traditional Huichol art to vibrant textiles, these souvenirs provide a tangible link to Sayulita's allure.

Huichol Art

Sacred and Colorful creations:

Huichol art is a distinct and sacred form of expression distinguished by brilliant colors and exquisite embroidery created by the indigenous Huichol people. Sayulita is a hub for collecting these one-of-a-kind pieces, giving tourists the opportunity to take home a cultural treasure.

Key creations:

- **Beaded Jewelry:** Huichol artists use small, bright beads to create magnificent jewelry items that typically feature traditional symbols and spiritual elements.

- **Yarn Paintings:** "nierikas," or intricate yarn paintings, depict the Huichol worldview and are frequently created during ceremonial rites.

- **Beaded Sculptures:** Three-dimensional sculptures of animals and spiritual symbols display the careful beadwork for which Huichol art is famous.

Appreciating Huichol Art:

- **Symbolism:** Many Huichol crafts are rich with symbolism, symbolizing aspects from nature, spirituality, and the Huichol people's cultural past.

- **Support Authenticity:** When purchasing Huichol art, consider purchasing directly from craftspeople or reputable galleries to assure authenticity and to support the artists and their communities.

Textiles and Clothing

Bohemian Chic Finds:

The bohemian spirit of Sayulita is reflected in its textiles and clothing offers. The town's shops offer a combination of classic Mexican aesthetics with current trends, from flowy beachwear to beautifully embroidered fabrics.

Key offerings:

- **Embroidered Blouses and Dresses**: Visit boutiques that sell wonderfully embroidered blouses and dresses, which frequently reflect the brilliant colors and exquisite designs of Mexican embroidery.

- **Handwoven Shawls & Scarves**: Popular souvenirs are handwoven textiles such as shawls and scarves, which are noted for their craftsmanship and adaptability.

- **Bohemian beachwear:** Sayulita's seaside location inspires a variety of bohemian beachwear, such as airy kaftans, tie-dye sarongs, and comfy swimwear.

Fashion Tips:

- **Try Before You Buy:** Many Sayulita businesses invite customers to try on clothing before making a purchase. Accept the laid-back attitude and take your time discovering different styles.

- **Mix & Match:** Create a one-of-a-kind wardrobe by combining traditional Mexican textiles with modern pieces. Sayulita's fashion scene encourages varied and individual looks.

One-of-a-kind Keepsakes

Sayulita's Memorable Tokens:

For those looking for souvenirs that capture the soul of Sayulita, the town has a selection of unusual goods that go beyond the ordinary. These keepsakes, which range from handcrafted trinkets to personalized art works, serve as lasting reminders of your experience in this charming coastal town.

Important mementos:

- **Personalized Artwork:** Many local artists provide personalized artwork, such as paintings or drawings that express the character of Sayulita. Consider commissioning a work that speaks to your experience.

- **Ceramics and pottery:** Sayulita is home to skilled ceramic artists. Handcrafted pottery, such as mugs, plates, and ornamental objects, provides for unique and useful souvenirs.

- **Local Photography:** Help local photographers capture the beauty of Sayulita. Prints or digital downloads of stunning photographs can add a touch of the town's sceneries to your house.

Keepsake tips:

- **Inquire about the tales:** When purchasing one-of-a-kind keepsakes, inquire about the tales behind the pieces from the artisans or makers. Learning about the motivation and the process enriches the keepsake.

- **Packaging and Care:** Take into account the fragility or unique care needs of your chosen treasure. Some items may require special attention during transportation to ensure they arrive in perfect condition.

Conclusion:

Sayulita's shopping environment reflects the town's vibrant culture, fusing traditional Mexican craftsmanship with modern bohemian flair. Whether you're looking for authentic gifts like Huichol paintings and textiles or exploring the lively Sayulita Mercado, each shopping experience in Sayulita is a trip into the heart of the town's creativity and culture.

You'll not only bring home tangible memories but also a piece of Sayulita's colorful character as you weave through markets, discover hidden boutiques, and select keepsakes that resonate with your adventure, creating a lasting connection to this coastal gem.

Chapter 9

PRACTICAL INFORMATION

Sayulita is more than just beautiful beaches and colorful culture.

In Chapter 9, we go over practical facts to guarantee that your stay is not only enjoyable but also smooth. This chapter covers everything you need to know about Sayulita, from communication basics to critical services and sustainable travel practices.

Communication and Connectivity

Keeping in Touch in Paradise:

While Sayulita provides a respite from the hustle and bustle, staying connected is nevertheless necessary for a variety of reasons, from staying in touch with loved ones to learning about local attractions. This section discusses Sayulita's communication environment, including internet and phone services, as well as Wi-Fi hotspots.

Phone and Internet Services

Options for Connectivity:

Sayulita offers a variety of internet and phone service choices to keep you connected during your stay. Understanding the available services and making informed decisions ensures that communication runs well.

Cellular Services:

- **Telcel:** Telcel is a well-known Mexican cellular service provider with extensive coverage in Sayulita. To gain access to dependable mobile data and call services, purchase a local SIM card for your unlocked phone.

- **Movistar:** Another cellular network that operates in Sayulita, providing SIM cards to guests seeking local access.

Internet Services:

Local Internet Providers: Some hotels and businesses provide Wi-Fi through local internet providers. For more information on connectivity, inquire about the internet services offered at your stay.

Visitors Should Know:

- **Local SIM Cards:** If you want to use cellular data substantially during your stay, consider getting a local SIM card upon arrival. This is a low-cost method of staying connected.

- **Wi-Fi Considerations:** While Wi-Fi is generally available in Sayulita, connectivity might be inconsistent. If you need constant internet access during your visit, check with your lodging about the quality and availability of Wi-Fi.

Wi-Fi Access Points

Beyond Accommodations, Connectivity:

Wi-Fi hotspots dot Sayulita, allowing travelers to stay connected while touring the town. These hotspots provide handy connectivity alternatives in a variety of settings, including cafes and public spaces.

Restaurants and cafes:

- **El Espresso:** Not only does this popular coffee shop provide delicious coffee, but it also has stable Wi-Fi, making it an ideal site for remote work or casual browsing.

- **Don Pedro's Restaurant and Bar:** Dine on the beach while remaining connected with Wi-Fi at Don Pedro's. The gorgeous setting of the restaurant enhances the whole experience.

Public spaces:

- **Sayulita Plaza:** The central plaza of the town is a hive of activity and a popular gathering place. It frequently has free Wi-Fi, allowing tourists to check their emails or share their Sayulita experiences online.

- **Beachfront Wi-Fi:** Some coastal places provide Wi-Fi connection, allowing you to enjoy the sun and surf while being connected digitally.

Wi-Fi tips:

- **Purchase Vouchers:** Wi-Fi connection in some establishments, particularly cafes, may require the purchase of a voucher or a minimum spend. Before using the internet, confirm the terms with the staff.

- **Outdoor Workspaces:** Take use of the Wi-Fi-enabled outdoor places to enjoy the beautiful Sayulita weather while remaining productive or connected.

Essential Services

Taking Care of Yourself:

Understanding where key services are located is critical for a worry-free visit. This section discusses medical facilities and emergency contacts to ensure you're prepared for any unanticipated circumstances.

Medical facilities

Sayulita Medical Care:

While Sayulita is a relatively secure place, knowing about nearby medical facilities might bring piece of mind. Knowing where to turn for medical aid in the event of an emergency or small health condition is critical.

Playa Sayulita Hospital:

Location: Ave. Revolucion, Sayulita

Contact: +52 329 291 3628

Sayulita Red Cross:

Location: Calle Manuel Rodriguez Sanchez 11, Sayulita

Contact: +52 329 291 6642

Pharmacies:

Farmacia Nayarit: Located in the town center, this pharmacy provides a range of over-the-counter medications and basic healthcare supplies

Health Tips:

- **Travel Insurance:** Consider obtaining travel insurance that covers medical emergencies. Check with your provider to ensure coverage for Sayulita healthcare treatments.

- **Pharmacy Hours:** Confirm pharmacy hours, especially if you require drugs after usual business hours.

Police and Emergency Contact

Assuring Safety:

While Sayulita is recognized for its welcoming atmosphere, knowing emergency contacts and local authorities gives an extra layer of security to your vacation.

Emergency Services:

Emergency Contact (General): 911

Sayulita Police (Non-Emergency): +52 329 291 3658

Safety Tips:

- **Save Local Numbers:** Save local emergency phone numbers in your phone for easy access. This ensures that you can reach out quickly in the event of an emergency.

- **Share Your Itinerary:** Inform someone about your plan and expected return time if you are participating in outdoor activities or excursions.

Sustainable Travel Practices

Respecting Sayulita's Ecosystem:

Sayulita's natural beauty is a treasure that must be protected. Adopting sustainable travel practices guarantees that your vacation benefits the environment and the local community.

Sustainable Tourism

Making a Positive Difference:

Responsible tourism is important to sustainable travel. You contribute to Sayulita's long-term well-being by adopting behaviors that reduce your environmental imprint and assist the local community.

Waste Management:

- **Use Reusable Items:** Carry a reusable water bottle and shopping bag to reduce your use of single-use plastic.

- **Proper waste Disposal:** Place rubbish in designated bins and, if available, follow recycling rules.

Cultural Respect:

- **Respect Local Customs:** Learn about and respect local customs and traditions. When visiting religious or cultural sites, dress modestly.

- **Support Local companies:** Make purchases from local companies, marketplaces, and craftsmen to directly benefit the neighborhood.

Eco-Friendly Initiatives

Protecting Sayulita's Ecosystem:

Sayulita has several eco-friendly projects and measures in place to conserve its natural resources. Understanding and supporting these efforts promotes a more sustainable and environmentally conscientious travel experience.

Sayulita Turtle conservation:

Participate in Nest Releases: Sayulita has a turtle conservation initiative. Look for ways to engage in nest releases and contribute to conservation initiatives.

Clean-up Days in the Community:

join in Local Initiatives: Keep up to date on any community clean-up events or environmental initiatives taking place during your visit. Participating in these activities helps to keep the community clean.

Sustainable Accommodations:

Choose Eco-Friendly lodgings: Some Sayulita lodgings adopt eco-friendly techniques such as water conservation, energy efficiency, and trash reduction. Consider staying in places that are committed to sustainability.

Conclusion

The ninth chapter, Practical Information, serves as a comprehensive guide to traversing Sayulita with ease and responsibility. This chapter covers the fundamentals for a worry-free visit, from staying connected with cellular and Wi-Fi services to safeguarding your well-being with information on medical facilities and emergency contacts. Furthermore, by adopting sustainable travel practices and supporting local projects, you help to preserve Sayulita's natural beauty and cultural diversity.

As you tour this seaside paradise armed with practical knowledge, you will not only have a pleasant journey but will also have a good impact on the community and the environment, forming a harmonious relationship with Sayulita's energetic spirit.

Chapter 10

SAMPLE ITINERARIES FOR DIFFERENT KINDS OF TRAVELERS

Sayulita has a wide range of experiences, making it a perfect location for a wide range of people, from beachgoers to cultural explorers. We give curated sample itineraries for various types of travelers in this chapter, ensuring that everyone can make the most of their time in this delightful coastal town.

Please keep in mind that the itineraries are adaptable and can be changed based on your own interests and the length of your stay.

Beach Bliss Retreat

For Sunseekers and Relaxation Enthusiasts

Day 1: Arrival and Beach Relaxation

- Arrive at Sayulita and check into your beachside lodging.
- Spend the afternoon relaxing on Playa Sayulita, taking in the sun, waves, and laid-back beach vibe.
- **Evening:** Dine at a beachside restaurant while watching the sunset over the Pacific.

Day 2: Sand and Surf

- Take a surf lesson or hire a paddleboard in the morning to explore the waves.
- **Afternoon:** Unwind on Playa de los Muertos, which is noted for its peaceful atmosphere and beautiful sands.
- **Evening:** Visit coastal bars for a relaxed supper and drinks.

Day 3: Hidden Gems

- **Morning:** For a more isolated experience, visit secret beaches such as Playa Carricitos or Playa Patzcuaro.
- **Afternoon:** Pamper yourself with a seaside massage or yoga session.
- Dinner at a seashore seafood restaurant in the evening.

Cultural Explorer's Journey

For History and Art Lovers

Day 1: Sayulita Orientation

- Arrive at a strategically situated hotel or vacation rental and check in.
- Visit Sayulita Pueblo, the town's central square, and local art galleries displaying regional and indigenous artwork.
- **Evening:** Dine at a local restaurant serving authentic Mexican cuisine.

Day 2: Historic Tour

- **Morning:** Take a walking tour of Sayulita's historic landmarks, including the Nuestra Seora de Guadalupe church.
- **Afternoon:** Tour the Sayulita Cemetery to learn about local customs.
- Attend a cultural event or a live music performance in the evening.

Day 3: Art and Crafts

- **Morning:** Visit Huichol art galleries and watch artists create beautiful beadwork.
- **Afternoon:** Attend an art workshop or class in your area to make your own masterpiece.
- Dinner at a classic Mexican restaurant in the evening.

Adventure Seeker's Expedition

For Thrill Seekers and Outdoor Enthusiasts

Day 1: Arrival and Adrenaline Rush

- Arrive and check into a hotel close to the adventurous activities.
- **Afternoon:** Begin with a rainforest zip-lining excursion.
- **Evening:** Unwind with a substantial lunch at a nearby restaurant.

Day 2: ATV and Jungle Exploration

- **Morning:** Go on an ATV excursion through the jungle and along the coast.
- **Afternoon:** Take a cool plunge in a hidden waterfall or natural pool.
- Dinner at a coastal restaurant with a view in the evening.

Day 3: Ocean Excursion

- **Morning:** Depending on the season, go on a boat excursion for snorkeling, fishing, or whale viewing.
- **Afternoon:** Relax on a secluded cove with a beach picnic or seafood lunch.
- **Evening:** Toast your eventful voyage with a beach bonfire at twilight.

Family-Friendly Fiesta

For Families with Children and Multigenerational Travelers

Day 1: Arrival and Family Activities

- Look for family-friendly lodging with kid-friendly features.
- **Afternoon:** Spend the day at the beach with your family, building sandcastles and playing beach games.
- **Evening:** Select a restaurant with a relaxing ambiance that is appropriate for families.

Day 2: Sayulita Exploration

- **Morning:** Explore Sayulita Pueblo, including the center plaza and souvenir shopping.
- **Afternoon:** Unwind at a family-friendly beach club with kid-friendly activities.
- **Evening:** Dinner at a restaurant with a varied menu that caters to all preferences.

Day 3: Nature and Wildlife

- For a family adventure, visit a wildlife refuge or go on a guided nature walk in the morning.
- **Afternoon:** Have a picnic in a nearby park or on the beach.
- **Evening:** Finish the day with a family movie night or ice cream.

Romantic Getaway

For Couples and Honeymooners

Day 1: Arrival and Sunset Peace

- Consider staying in a romantic boutique hotel or a beachside home.
- **Evening:** Take a sunset walk along the beach before enjoying a romantic supper at a beachside restaurant.

Day 2: Waterfront Romance

- **Morning:** Take a couples' surf instruction or relax with a couples' massage on the beach.

- **Afternoon:** Have a private seaside picnic or discover hidden coves with your friends.
- **Evening:** Dine in a candlelight restaurant.

Day 3: Romance in Sayulita

- Hand in hand, stroll through the lovely streets of Sayulita Pueblo in the morning.
- **Afternoon:** Go to a local spa for a couples' massage.
- **Evening:** Go to a rooftop restaurant for a romantic dinner under the stars.

Tips for Planning Your Trip:

- **Organize your interests:** Determine your trip group's major interests and prioritize activities that match with those interests.

- **Balance Relaxation and Exploration:** Maintain a healthy balance of beach relaxation and cultural or adventure pursuits.

- **Consider Travel Partners:** Make the itinerary to suit everyone in your trip party's preferences and energy levels.

- **Local Events and Festivals:** Check the local events calendar for any festivals or events taking place during your stay and plan accordingly.

These sample itineraries are intended to inspire and guide all types of travelers through the numerous experiences available in Sayulita. Feel free to personalize and combine activities to create a bespoke experience that reflects the essence of this wonderful coastal town.

Sayulita welcomes you with open arms and a plethora of alternatives for an unforgettable travel experience, whether you're looking for relaxation, cultural immersion, adventure, or romance.

REFLECTING ON YOUR SAYULITA EXPERIENCE

Take a moment to think on the tapestry of experiences that have woven together to create enduring memories as your journey in Sayulita comes to a conclusion. Sayulita's gorgeous beaches, rich culture, and friendly spirit create an indelible impression on any traveler who is fortunate enough to visit its shores.

Embracing the Laid-Back vibe: Sayulita's allure stems from its laid-back feel, where time seems to slow down and you can fully immerse yourself in the rhythm of the Pacific. Whether you spent relaxed days on the beach, explored Sayulita Pueblo's colorful streets, or trekked into the nearby forests, each moment adds to the unique mosaic of your Sayulita experience.

Cultural Tapestry: Sayulita's cultural diversity, with its indigenous traditions and creative flair, provides a unique backdrop for your journey narrative. Sayulita's cultural tapestry becomes a thread woven into the fabric of your recollections, from discovering the delicate embroidery of Huichol artists to tasting the flavors of traditional Mexican food.

Connecting with Nature: Sayulita's natural splendor, from its clean beaches to its lush jungles, urges you to have a deep connection with the environment. Whether you went on outdoor excursions, saw sea turtle hatchlings released, or simply enjoyed the peaceful sound of the waves, your connection with nature in Sayulita attests to the town's ecological allure.

Farewell and Future Adventures

As you say goodbye to Sayulita, remember that the magic of this coastal paradise will live on in your heart. Memories of brilliant sunsets, the taste of real street tacos, and laughter shared with fellow visitors become tangible treasures. Sayulita becomes more than a vacation spot; it becomes a part of your personal journey.

Taking a Piece of Sayulita with You: Take a piece of Sayulita with you on your future journeys. Let these memories serve as portals to the moments you treasured in this beachside haven, whether it's a piece of Huichol art, a melody from a local performance, or the warmth of the Sayulita sun on your skin.

Open the Door to Future Explorations: Sayulita is a gateway to discovery, and each goodbye opens the door to future adventures. The globe is big and full of destinations awaiting discovery. Carry Sayulita's essence — its easygoing nature, cultural depth, and natural beauty — with you on future excursions, knowing that the traveler's heart is always fired by the prospect of the unknown.

When you say goodbye to Sayulita, you're not simply leaving a place; you're carrying the essence of a place that welcomed you with open arms with you. May your trips be filled with the same warmth, curiosity, and admiration that Sayulita has bestowed upon you. For the time being, farewell, and may your future experiences be as enthralling as your time in this coastal paradise.

Useful Phrases and Vocabulary

A rudimentary familiarity of local idioms and vocabulary will enrich your trip experience in the vibrant tapestry of Sayulita. Here are some phrases to assist you navigate conversations and immerse yourself in local culture:

- Hola: Hello
- Gracias: Thank you

- Por favor: Please
- Sí: Yes
- No: No
- ¿Cuánto cuesta?: How much does it cost?
- ¿Dónde está...?: Where is...?
- Me gusta: I like it
- Delicioso: Delicious
- Playa: Beach
- Mercado: Market
- Restaurante: Restaurant
- Baño: Bathroom

Using these terms to interact with locals demonstrates your admiration for the culture and adds a personal touch to your Sayulita trip.

Packing Checklist

Pack carefully to have a smooth and pleasurable stay in Sayulita. Here's a list to help you get ready for your coastal adventure:

- **Light clothing:** Pack breathable and light clothing appropriate for warm temperatures.

- **Swimsuits:** Sayulita's beaches are a must-see, so bring yours.

- **Sun Protection:** Bring sunscreen, a wide-brimmed hat, and sunglasses to protect yourself from the sun.

- **Comfortable footwear:** Sandals or comfortable shoes are ideal for touring the town and beaches.

- **Reusable Water Bottle:** Stay hydrated, especially in hot weather.

- **Daypack or beach bag:** Carry essentials for day trips and beach adventures with a daypack or beach bag.

- **Spanish Phrasebook:** basic phrasebook will help you improve your communication skills in Spanish.

- **Travel Adapter:** Make sure your devices can be charged using the local power outlets.

- **Travel Insurance:** Be prepared for the unexpected by purchasing comprehensive travel insurance.

- **First Aid Kit:** Include basic drugs, bandages, and any personal prescription meds in your first aid kit.

- **Camera or Smartphone:** Capture the grandeur of Sayulita and its surrounds with your camera or smartphone.

- **Travel Documents:** Bring your passport, identification, travel insurance information, and any relevant permissions.

- **Local Currency:** Keep some Mexican pesos on hand for modest transactions and tips.

- **Snorkeling Equipment:** If you intend to explore the aquatic environment, pack your snorkeling equipment.

Maps and Navigational Aids

With the use of maps and navigation materials, navigating Sayulita becomes easier. Here are some useful resources:

- **Offline Maps:** Download Sayulita offline maps to navigate without internet access.

- **Google Maps:** Use Google Maps for real-time navigation, restaurant reviews, and searching for points of interest.

- **Local Maps:** For a full overview of the town, pick up a local map at your hotel or tourist information center.

- **Navigation Apps:** Look into navigation apps that provide information about public transportation, walking routes, and local attractions.

With these resources at your disposal, you may confidently explore Sayulita, uncovering hidden gems and having a flawless vacation experience.

Made in the USA
Columbia, SC
17 December 2024

49631562R00109